Custom Shifting Cleaning and Organizing Company Presents: Home Energy

CHRISTYNA ERIN

Copyright © 2024 by Christyna Erin

All rights reserved.

In honor of...

This book is dedicated to my sister and best friend, Michelle. I know it wasn't easy sharing a room together in our childhood. We are so opposite in our styles as I was so busy and she likes it simple. It took me a long time to accept myself for who I am instead of comparing myself to what I should be. Here's to all the people who like their homes simple, and to those who like it "busy". We are all perfect just the way we are.

And to my dear friend Linda, who also owns a cleaning business. She has my back no matter what and believes in my crazy ideas. Cheers to being a little "extra".

Table of Contents

Part One

1. What is Custom Shifting — 1
2. Change What You Can — 5
3. Everyone IS Different — 15
4. Home Energy — 19
5. What you Want — 25
6. Assessing your space — 33
7. The What and the Way — 37
8. Organizing — 39
9. Prioritizing — 47
10. Decluttering — 51
11. Collecting vs Hoarding — 57
12. Letting Go — 63
13. Bringing it back — 81
14. Reasons we Don't do it — 87
15. Procrastinating — 93
16. Time Management — 97
17. Responsibilities and Obligations — 117
18. Setting Boundaries and creating Limits — 125

Part Two

19. Cleaning Style	133
20. Keeping it all clean	141
21. Tricks of the Trade	147
22. Cutting Corners	151
23. Products	159
24. Problem Areas	165
25. Our senses	171
26. Essential Oils	175
27. The Elements	179
28. Feng shui	183
29. Lighting	185
30. Colors	187
31. Motivation	189
32. Be Yourself	193
33. Resources and Research	195

Intro...

When I first started on my journey with Custom Shifting, I felt broken. I knew I needed change. I was always moving my house around trying to fix what was not right, not me. One day I realized it was me, not my house that was lost. One day I had looked around and my house was my inner mirror. I decided to change that, whatever I felt I could change, and then focus on what I needed more control of. I talked my way through my journey of finding who I am, what I like to do and who I was meant to be. I then had to change more than just my space. But the process is the same, it all starts with home energy. Once you can shift yourself, you can change anything...

I grew up on a dairy farm in Vermont. I come from a long line of hard workers. I am a hardworking Mom of three young kids, and I have multiple jobs. My passion lies in home design, redecorating, helping others and *Change*. I have always been a writer, but was too afraid to share my work with others. I believe anyone can learn to do anything themselves. My laundry still piles up sometimes. Please do not beat yourself up if your house is not perfect. No one is perfect. What we are striving for is acceptance and peace in our environment. If you are reading or listening to this, it probably means you are looking for some sort of change. And good for you for acting!

First off, I am not a perfect cleaner, or a perfect writer. If you're looking for a grammarly correct piece, I am not your girl. I do however shine at giving advice and helping others. The reason I wrote this workbook like this is because it is set up like a course, as if I am talking you through it. You investing in this course and having me help you to help yourself is so much more cost effective for you than hiring a professional to help you. You have" hired" out almost free now because you will do the work yourself as I walk you through it. So please consider my words as speech and not so much a typical written book, but the tools you will use to brainstorm and accomplish your own success.

My goal is to help people. I have always loved helping people, it makes me happy. I would love to teach you how you can accomplish for yourself what I do for others in my business. I organize, declutter, clean, and redecorate. Think of this book as a course, an outline for a new you. You can revisit and practice as much as you need to. The ultimate goal for this course is to help you do you and focus on you and your space

I am very experienced at both writing and cleaning so my advice is solid. I spent years learning how to dehoard, organize and clean efficiently in general. I own a cleaning business, but keep in mind that it is much easier to clean in my clients homes than my own. The reason being is that I become the *outside-in* view. I don't live there. It is easy to get distracted in our own homes and be "sight blind" to the truth. That being said, I can help you see from the outside as if I was there, so you can fix your own space.

I want to help people help themselves. Hire out for what you need to. And ask for help when you need to, but you can do so much of this yourself that I bet you will be shocked by the shifts that you are capable of. I am living proof of that. I believe in learning from other people's mistakes as well as our own, so that makes me the perfect teacher. I've spent over a decade in home reconstruction and demo, with most of it doing myself. Tiling is one of my passions, as is painting and refinishing. I'm a designer, a thinker and a do-er.

There is more than one way to do everything. Repeat that. More than one way to do everything. This thought is super important in this journey. So much of the time we believe that we are not doing something right. There is always a different way to do something. So that means that your way can and will work if it gets you to the end result that you strive for. We were always taught that if we don't do this, then we can't do that. That we have to do this for that to happen. It's simply just not true. Results can be achieved using a different method. Always. Don't be afraid to be you and realize what you want and get it. We will go through that in our course.

I refer to "space" as anywhere you live. It could be a room you are renting, an apartment, a house you own. But wherever you live, is your own space. To make it yours. I advise you to please do the activities because that is how you'll figure out what is best for you. Keep a journal of your responses for change happens all the time and you can remind yourself what you need to if it is documented.

This workbook uses pronouns such as "you", "I", and "we". The reason is because I am talking to you in this book and WE can do this together. You got this. Write your answers to every question and do not give up, I promise it is worth it. You are worth it, I am worth it, and We are worth it.

Part One of this book is on to establish the space meant for you.
Part Two of this book is on to maintain the space meant for you.

So grab a pen and let's get going!

Chapter 1
What is Custom Shifting

I started my business with the idea to help people change their space and celebrate their differences in an environment where they could feel comfortable to do so. I had been cleaning in some way professionally for twenty years and during my lifetime experience waitressing had interacted with so many different personalities.

One of my favorite activities is rearranging houses to create change. This emotionally helps to balance what is going on in our life that we cannot change. The Shift is similar to people going to the hairdresser, which I am licensed to do as well. We feel better about ourselves when we change or control our lives, especially when we feel out of control for other reasons.

I only advertised as "shifting home energy" and making positive changes in people's environments. I started off by organizing and decluttering many homes, however eventually all my clients wanted me to clean and maintain their spaces. I realized how a clean home affected their energy. When I first started out in business, I would do anything for anybody. I had only a few home staging jobs which I loved so much, and even hold a certificate for. If I was asked to mop a floor, I would pick up poop on the floor. If I was asked to clean the bathroom, I would rid it of mold, which I am highly allergic to. I did not set boundaries or limits for myself, which I will go into practicing later.

I wanted to help people and turned no one down, even if they could not afford it. Eventually a few years later, I realized I was not practicing respect for myself and not in business for what I wanted to do anymore. I felt like more of a "maid" than a home energy consultant.

When I was helping someone change their home, it was very emotional and personal for them. So many people are secretly embarrassed to ask for help when they need it, so I thought of a different way I help people without disrespecting myself. That is when I decided I could just teach people how to do it themselves.

My turning point was a class I was asked to teach at a local library. I wrote this book off of what I taught. I was passionate about change and it was exciting for me. They asked me to teach a class on minimalism. I refused and said I didn't believe there is only one way to be or live. The director agreed to allow me to instruct the class the way I believed. I believe in differences and acceptance for those differences.

I had much more than a class written at this point, so I turned my instruction manual into a workbook. Teaching yourself is better than hiring me personally, because you can work at your pace and privacy. Your very own "Custom Shifting" will be a rewarding journey where you choose the end result. I have heard from many people how I have changed their lives, but I was just hoping for their success. If only I could care for everyone and at the same time, care for myself, this book is that. Thank you so much for the journey. I am proud of you.

This book is designed for you to fill in your answers to the questions, please do so. To get your answers and successful path, simply read and answer the questions in this workbook honestly and then reflect. There is no way to fail and so much to learn and gain. Eliminate Doubt from your mind. You will succeed at this, and I promise by the end of this course, you will have the tools to change more than just your environment. Your *change* can spiral a lifetime of happiness, not just in your home, but in your life. Accept yourself and together we can change every single "I can't" into "I did it".

My whole life I tried to change, change everything around me without first changing that way I thought about myself. *Custom Shifting* is a change that is Custom to you. You reached out for a reason. Read the book to the end and use the energy as power. Power to believe, power to change, power to be you. You do not have to settle, you do not have to suffer, you do not have to blame and be hurt. You deserve to be happy, to be safe and have control of your life. Start with your home, find your happy place. I am honored to be with you on this journey. I have been there and I see you, I understand and I am here for you. Change can seem hard, but the journey is worth the growth. Start believing you can "Change what you can", because you can!

My whole life I was waiting for the one person to believe in me to come along, until I realized that one person was me. I want to help you believe in yourself. Save yourself the time and energy and invest in *you*. Step One: Take the advice. This book was a small fee, but the advice is free and priceless. I have the best advice because I have made all the mistakes already and learned from them, and my heart is pure. Let my experience help you recover. This will all make sense at the end of the course. The "ah-hah" moments are worth its weight in gold. Saving time, means saving energy, and saving energy on lack means more energy for the most important.

I seriously want to help people with just the cost you already spent on this book, so please help yourself. I tried to help everyone I came into contact with when running and owning my cleaning business. My journey and experience with everything changed my perspective on how I looked at the importance of a happy home. I want my mistakes to be well spent. That is my motto, "Change what you can". I have changed... and so can *you*.

I even struggled so hard to release this book, thinking it was "Not good enough". My mind still goes back there and I have to fight it, but I am working on it. And I know what works now. I have learned about myself and what makes me happy, and I am not afraid to do me and I love what I am doing now. So can you...

Chapter 2
Change What You Can

My motto for my business is *"Change What You Can."* Think about it, there are so many things we cannot change, so it makes sense to change what we can. I bet we all wished we had a magic wand that we could wave that could change a cold rainy day into a beautiful sunny day. But we can't change that. Nor can we change the mind of a coworker that is direct on not coming in for a shift. We can try, but ultimately we can only change what we can. So the power lies in what we can change instead of worrying about what cannot be changed directly by us.

A different way to look at this is to *Control What You Can.* A true statement that I repeat to my children is that we can only control ourselves. We cannot control others. We can not control the weather, or certain events. There are a million things in our lives that can make us feel out of control. A person can however, control themselves. Most of us can control our reaction and emotion and therefore, our situational outcome to a circumstance. We have that control.

Our emotions place a huge impact on our energy. If we feel good, our energy is good. If we are angry, we can put off "negative vibes". Feeling displaced can set off a mood that makes us feel like we don't belong. We can control *our* emotions and reactions to *others'* emotions, so therefore our energy. A huge part of our happiness can be how we feel in our environment. How the energy in our home feels. It is our space. And should be our happy place. How we feel when we are home, and how our home feels to us.

> *The secret is to ask yourself: How does my home currently make me feel? Then establish that balance from what we have and what we want.*

Our home environment is something most adults *can* control. Perhaps as kids we felt that we didn't have much control over our environment. When I did this class at our local library, I had a lady respond that she wanted a new apartment in general. That she didn't like her apartment at all. At that time there just happened not to be any apartments for rent, so she had to make do with her current rental. She just couldn't control that part. But what she did with space in that apartment to make it better suit her needs, was something she could control. Getting a new place was on her wish list, but changing what she could at the time with her current space, was something she could control. Perhaps you have a roommate that drives you crazy and you have to live with them until other shifts happen in your life.

Brainstorming ways to change the situation to make it more comfortable could be something you could control. If they are too loud, you could get headphones and listen to an audio book when they are home. The point is that there are so many things we can't control, but more that we can change if we can think differently about the situation.

We can assert control in our environment. We have the power to change what we can. One of the easiest things we can control is our environment. Start by making a list. It will help so much. One column is "things I cannot control", and the other is "what I can change".

In this example, using control and change in a similar context will help to better understand the concept of the power we have for change. There is power to control the environment in which we live. This list could be anything in life. It will help you define some answer to a situation you'd like to adjust in your favor.

On a piece of paper, in this book or in a notebook, journal or computer, make two columns. At the top of the first one, write "What I cannot Control in life". At the top of the other column, write "What I can Change in life".

Examples are:

<u>What I cannot control:</u>
   The weather
   Reactions of other people
   Missing a day of work from being sick
   Physical traits, i.e. my height

<u>What I can Change:</u>
   How prepared I am for the weather
   How I react to other peoples reaction
   How I handle a situation or feeling good about my choice
   Choosing my hairstyle

Of course the list can go on for quite some time. Remember there is always a different way to approach something. There is always another way to think about a situation or a different way to change the outcome.

My outdoor-type cat growls at me sometimes when I make her stay inside overnight. I *could* choose to feel anxious, scared or angry, but I laugh at her. I accept the cat the way she is, appreciate it. I know that I can't change her behavior, unless I change the cause. I am not willing to change the cause, so I accept it. But, I can always change my outlook. Change What You Can, and you can always change your outlook.

Custom Shifting Cleaning and Organizing Company Presents: Home Energy

CONTROL AND CHANGE – LIFE IN GENERAL

<u>What I cannot *Control*</u>:

<u>What I can *Change*</u>:

Now I want you to think about your environment. We decided that we could have control in other areas of our life. There are things that we have the power to change. Our space is the easiest to change. It may take longer to get a new apartment or home. Maybe a new job. Or move to a new state, if the weather is a concern for happiness. But anything can change your space and could be done right away to change your energy and thus, change your mood. The new list is for our space. Our home.

What I can't control, and What I can change. Everyone's list will be different because no one has the same space or environment. This is why it is important that you do the brainstorming yourself following the examples because I can't tell you to move your fridge if you don't have the electrical plug in to do so. This course will help you help yourself.

On a piece of paper, in this book, or in a notebook, journal, or computer, make two columns. On the top of the first one, write: "What I can't control in my environment. At the top of the other column, write: "What I can change in my space". I can change the color of my walls, because I own my home. Every single person's list will be different depending on what they have for a space and what they want out of their space. But everyone will have something on the list of what they can change.

Examples are:
What I can't control:
    The size of my kitchen
    My neighbors
What I can Change:
    The colors of my walls
    The amount of my clutter
    The layout of my bedroom

Custom Shifting Cleaning and Organizing Company Presents: Home Energy

CONTROL AND CHANGES IN OUR ENVIRONMENT:

What I cannot *Control* in my Environment:

What I can *Change* in my Space:

Really think about everything that you can change and focus on that. I bet there is more that you can change than you thought. Let's play with this idea for a minute. Almost every night, most of us all have a sink full of dirty dishes or would have if we didn't do them as we went. If we let them pile up for days, we probably would not have any clean dishes to use later. So we wash them. That is a change we make to solve a potential problem that would affect our energy. Without any clean dishes, we couldn't make dinner. It seems like a small change, but it is so effective. And makes a big difference in our life.

We actually do so many changes without thinking about them because it has become a habit for us. I bet you wash your laundry so you can have clean clothes. You probably buy toothpaste when you run out so you have clean teeth. Those changes shift the energy of how you would feel if you didn't do those tasks.

I bet we can all make a list of the changes we do everyday to better our lives or get us to how we want to feel. We prevent things, we change the outcome. I brush my daughter's hair so it doesn't get caught in a big dread of tears. It doesn't sound like a "change", but consider the outcome if i didn't. I changed my energy by preventing something that would've ended in a mess. Try making a list of everything you already do in your daily life to create change for the better. You will prove to yourself that not only are you capable of change, you are good at it.

Examples of activities that change our live for the better:
Changing our sheets so we feel fresh
Taking the trash out to prevent stink and bacteria
Paying our electric bill so we have lights

Custom Shifting Cleaning and Organizing Company Presents: Home Energy

    You are capable of change and preventing larger, more undesirable outcomes. If only all tasks in our environment came as easy and true to nature as taking a shower or bath. We are going to dive deep into time management, how to organize our space, decluttering and turning our space into something we can't wait to thrive in. You have the power to control your personal environment and change!

Custom Shifting Cleaning and Organizing Company Presents: Home Energy

EVERYTHING I DO IN A DAY:
(Accomplish)

Chapter 3
Everyone IS Different

I believe this so wholeheartedly that I have this phrase tattooed on my forearm. Everyone is so Different. This key to understanding people applies to every situation all the time. Understanding this concept is so important for change to work in this transition. Have you ever gone into someone's clean and uncluttered and vacant home and thought, "Wow! I wish I had a house like that?" Do you really think so? Let's find out, I'll explain.

Everyone's house is different. Their needs and wants all vary greatly. Every single one of us has a different house with different stuff, different people and different energy. It's more important to focus on what you like about the home that you aspire to, the adjectives. Is it clean, simple or very decorated? How does that home of your dreams make you feel? Peaceful or calm? Notice those describing words of the home you like.

Take note of the way you would like to feel in your home. Imagine your dream home. Picture yourself in that home, now imagine the way that home makes you *feel*. You will want different things in your home than anyone else, because you are different.

We can appreciate the beauty in another space, and judge its value as determined for the situation that it is in. The museum looks great plastered in artifacts, but not so much our home. Great spaces work best in a place where they suit the individual.

Beautifully carved windows in front of an amazing view is certainly something to awe in. Not so much facing a brick wall though.

You can figure out exactly what you want from establishing who you are. Our individual lifestyles and personalities should reflect who we are and what we want from life. The space should reflect who you are and truly make you happy. Everyone will want different things. I won't tell you to place elephants around your house to make you happy, collecting elephants is my thing. Let's figure out your thing and do you.

It would actually be horrible if everyone was forced to live in the same exact carbon copy of a space. An over-decorated place would make some people feel anxious, and a vacant home would make some people feel lonely and cold. We all do have individual styles and differences and they should be celebrated in our freedom to do so. We are lucky we have the choice to express our own freedom in our space without worrying about being judged. The freedom we have as adults today is very exciting and that right should be practiced.

I've got a quick four step process that helps determine what we want from our space and how to achieve it with balance, happiness and success. It will change your perspective on who you strive to be. Deciding and prioritizing your space around who you are will shift the energy in your environment. Be different and love who you are-so you can love your space.

Forgiveness is a huge step in feeling happy and peaceful. Holding grudges will weigh down your energy, so please try to practice forgiveness on yourself as well. As you start to change, remember not to be hard on yourself. In the never-ending construction of my old house, I always told my carpenters that the idea was "better than it was." Focus on the progress and how far you have come. Nothing in this world is perfect, but everything is changing everyday and never being how it was.

You will notice the phrase "is different" over and over in this book. The repetition is on purpose and I almost omitted it, but I want to drill this point across. The reason this is so important is because we have become a comparison society. There is such pressure to have what we think others have, or be what we think they are.

Should we all be thin, trendy and a million "likes" on social media? No, actually being a leader and setting the trend for loving yourself is the most attractive quality out there. The pride and strength to be yourself. If you have big hair and like it, rock the big hair. If you are tall, rock it. If you are an artist or doctor, own that. We might as well be ourselves. Some people are thin, but we do not have to be them unless we are.

The point is to celebrate differences. Not one body and mind is like another, so we shouldn't try to be like anyone but ourselves. The combination of our personal body and mind will never exist again in history. So, most of our energy should be focused on who we are and what we want to do.

Honestly jealousy is a lack of self worth. It is deciding you are not good enough, and someone is better. Jealousy is not realizing how unique and special you are and accepting your gifts and using who you are as an advantage. Jealousy is toxic. Being grateful for who you are eliminates that. I want you to repeat over and over to yourself that you are you for a reason. Learning to accept and love yourself is hard, but it does kill envy. I am lucky I never struggled with envy, but I struggled with the lack of self-esteem.

It took me a lifetime to love myself and accept myself. I'm sharing what I learned from my mistakes to save you time and energy.

The strength in realizing the dreams and hobbies we had as kids could still exist now. The limits are only there if we put them there ourselves. We live in a choice society right now and should exercise that right. And we can also choose to change.

Chapter 4
Home Energy

What is home energy? Home energy is the way you feel in your space. The same way I talked about how a bad mood can become contagious to others from letting off a "bad vibe", your home can create and let off energy too. Have you ever noticed how a bad smell of an unkept cat box can trigger your mood or shift your vibe? Can you concentrate on your homework if there's a ton of noises all around all happening at once? Does the smell of fresh baked cookies make you feel a little hungry? It's all about the mood your environment is creating in your energy.

Feeling is reacting and reacting is feeling. This is so powerful. If you feel that there are a million chores to do in your home, working from home will be hard. I would be so distracted if I attempted to focus my attention on remaining in the same spot for an extended period of time and not thinking about the laundry, the dog, the phone calls, and the chores that I feel I should complete right then. I would be distracted and uneasy and not crossing off my to do list would raise my anxiety. My energy would be directly affected by my un-done tasks if I was home not completing them. That is me and I am different.

The main point is that changing our home's energy will change the way we feel in our space. We can feel peace and look forward to going home and truly love ourselves in our environment because it is something we can have control over. Maybe you have a job you're not fond of and spend most of your week doing it. You should smile on your way home to your happy place and get excited when you enter. The chores you do to change the potential circumstances of a bad outcome will not seem so daunting when you look forward to loving your space and know you are doing it for yourself.

How would a haunted house feel? A staged one on halloween or a home one on the horror movies? Not happy huh. More like fear, anxiety, willingness to escape, and uneasy energy. It's a pretty instant feeling. Have you ever gone to a funeral and felt sad the second you walked in the church? What about a packed arcade? Busy and loud and bright and energetic. Notice how the environment can change the way you feel.

Note how your home currently makes you feel. Is it busy, if so do you like being busy?

The important fact to remember is that your space only has to fit your energy and those who live there. Maybe you are busy. It is all about finding what makes you happy in your space.

What vibe do you think your space gives off? What words come to mind when you describe your current living situation, are they positive? If not, are you wondering how you can change that? Because you can!

We actually can change the energy, or the way our space feels to us. An environment with good energy actually feels good, no matter the personality type. Even as we sleep, it's important our space makes us feel good, safe and holds the trust to be ourselves and be free. If we feel positive in our environment, we are more likely to think positive thoughts. If we feel uneasy or unsafe in our home, we let off that energy or vibe into our home. Home should be our happy place. *A space of our own is our freedom and it should express who we are and who we want to be, not what we are afraid of or hide behind.*

Let's explain energy. An old lady in the grocery store makes eye contact with you, she smiles at you. What is your reaction? Most of the time, a person would automatically smile back. Her energy made you mirror her happiness. Her kindness was contagious. Your environment can act the same way. If the the vibe your current living situation is giving off to you personally is cold, uninviting, cluttered or messy, you're not feeling the smile from your environment to smile back. Without realizing it, you might feel unproductive, unclear, anxious, agitated, or nervous in your space. That is no way to feel in your "happy place". We should all feel happy in our happy place. We have the freedom to make our space our happy place and we should exercise that right.

Please just jot down a list of how your current environment makes you feel. This is energy. You know how calm feels. There's a big difference between how a hallmark movie makes someone feel and a horror movie. The feeling you get from each is different. What does your home make you feel? That is the energy you are giving off in your environment. I want you to think about how your space makes you feel right now. A sink full of dishes would make an OCD cleaning type feel very uneasy and restless. I will talk about that notion later. But notice your space and how it makes you feel, right now. Look around your home and access your "problem areas", your triggers.

Does your closet make you feel worried because there is not enough space?

Does your living room make you feel closed in because it seems small?

Is your bathroom a place of procrastination?

What energy do you feel in your home?

Are you always worried or upset in your home?
Or rushed or overwhelmed?

It's important to note how you currently feel in your home, but not be hard on yourself or get discouraged by your answers. Acknowledging your current feelings in your space is the first step to change. It is not your outcome or future. Your change is possible and will happen with your victory to realize you can control your environment.

Perhaps some rooms give off a different vibe to you than other spaces in your home. Listing the feeling associated with the different spaces will also help you determine where your focus needs to be first for change so your space meets your requirements.

Custom Shifting Cleaning and Organizing Company Presents: Home Energy

HOW DOES MY HOUSE MAKE ME FEEL?

Chapter 5
What you Want

Now the fun part...

Establishing good energy in your home is a matter of finding the right mental, physical and environmental balance of what you want, who you are and what you want to be. Your space is who you want to be and my space is who I want to be. It starts out that simple. It may seem like an easy question to some, but it is not always what we think at first. So, What do *you* want?

Follow this simple four step process to get your answer. Take your time on each step and think about the answers with the belief that it is truly possible. Do not limit your answers with disbelief or "but I can't have that". Answer honestly and dream big.

Step 1:

Write a list of adjectives that represent qualities you would like to see in your surroundings

The describing words that outline how your dream home would feel to you, what would describe your perfect environment:

My list went like this: Freedom, Acceptance, Flexibility, Safety, Comfort, Peace and Fun

THE FEELINGS I WANT MY HOUSE TO BE:(ADJECTIVES)

Step 2:

Make a list of who you are and what you love to do most. These are the verbs such as cooking, reading, exercising etc..

What action words best describe your personality and your passion for doing:

My list was: Making music, doing Arts and crafts, dancing and writing

THE ACTION OF WHO I AM (VERB)

Step 3:
Establish balance. Answer these questions:

Can you make a space in your environment for what makes you happy physically or mentally?

Is there a space in your home you have set aside for the actions you listed in step Two?

What is mentally standing in the way of environmental change? Example: No time to take care of clutter in your room to enjoy yoga?

What is physically standing in your way of achieving your optimal environment? Example: No table to draw for art.

Step 4:
Now we connect the dots. You've established:

What I want from your space

Who I want to be in your environment

What might be standing in the way of achieving that balance

Now, let's make a plan on how to get what you want out of your space. Everyone is different and every space is different. We know that. It is a matter of getting your personal space working for you. Most of the time, Step three of brainstorming comes up with some of the same categories. The challenges, the hurdles, the obstacles to overcome have something in common. We can learn to combat those excuses, instead of believing they are reasons.

Decluttering, redecorating, repositioning, rearranging and organizing can often bring solutions to our hurdles, bringing in new spaces and growth for change. These areas can shift the energy in the home. It is often not as hard as we think to organize and you are honestly going to look forward to the positive change that it brings.

Keep the adjectives you wrote down handy. Put the list on the fridge so you can check in with yourself and your space to make sure the changes you make reflect how you choose to feel in your home. The verbs in Step two describe the priorities you should make space for in your environment and your life. They are your passions and deserve the space in your life. These two steps are the most important part of change and being happy for who you are in your own space. Really think hard about choosing what is honest for you without telling yourself you can't have it. Because you can.

Two simple questions, "what do I like to do?", and "what makes me happy?" is the start of establishing positive energy in your space. Change is possible and it's already shifting with the honest answer of these questions.

I wrote "Freedom" on my list because who wouldn't want to feel Freedom in their home? The freedom to express myself and not be judged. The one place in my life I can let my guard down and be myself without fear of rejection. Freedom to design as I want, the freedom to sing and dance in my own space without embarrassment. Freedom to come and go as I please without asking permission. It's definitely important to me, safety for me is feeling freedom.

I want a space without the fear of being hurt or abused. I want a warm house with walls and a roof and a place where I can laugh when I want and cry when I want without anyone telling me no. I want a safe place. These adjectives were important qualities to me to have in my own space, so they immediately made my list. I wasn't always free or safe in my home, so my ideal happy place describes freedom and safety.

Everyone's list will be different because everyone is different. That is the point in having your own space and knowing it is *your* space. Remember we didn't get that choice as a child, our environment was made for us. We are lucky to have choices as adults, and even more lucky we are free to decide our lives. There are still many parts of the world, where expressing yourself, even in your space, feels impossible. So how lucky am I that I have a choice to decide? The easiest place to express yourself is in your own home. So our homes should be our happy place and reflect who we want to be and how we want to feel.

Custom Shifting Cleaning and Organizing Company Presents: Home Energy

Basically the process goes like this:

I want:

I am:

I need this for that to happen:

So I can do this to get that result::

It would be a great idea to put this list on your fridge for reference.

Chapter 6
Assessing your space

In our space we have things that are needed to survive comfortably. An easy starter is a bathroom. I think we can all agree having a bathroom is something we would like to keep in our home. Our kitchen to cook and eat, and a place to sleep and rest. The rest of our spaces are just extra. It's up to us individually as different people to make our priority lists of what else we would like from our space. If we like to entertain and cook for others, we might put a big table space on the priority list. If cuddling on the couch watching tv is a favorite pastime, then we might want a bigger space for a living area with a couch big enough for everyone to join in. All of our spaces will be different depending on our desires. It does not have to be traditional.

Remember your space can be whatever you decide, in any room of the house depending on your priorities. Your priorities will be the key to your success. You decide what is most important for your space in your home. If storing extra toilet paper is more important to you than having a place for your crafts, you decide. All spaces are different. Some of us just do not have the storage, and so that means we have to store less belongings. It is actually a blessing. Having a ton of storage space can end up being a problem for those of us who like to collect things we shouldn't hold to.

The important concept is to set a priority for the verbs in Step Two. I had Music on my list. I asked myself: So where in my house can I set aside a space for music? Where can I set aside a place for my art? What spaces are important in your own home?

Really take a look around and decide what spaces you have in your home. Does your furniture take up all the floor space you need to dance? What spaces do you need to satisfy your verbs that describe what you love to do? Making decisions like this one was easier when we were kids. We'd think that if we love legos, we would need a place to do legos. It was that simple to think. Now we shut that out with practical thoughts with "I can'ts". When actually we have way more freedom to change than we did as kids. You can in fact make a painting nook or reading corner. You just have to know what you want, and know what you already have to work with, then access what needs to be rearranged or changed to accomplish that. Maybe you still do like legos, and you can.

Start by accessing your current space. If you have a studio apartment, break down your space into sections. They may not be separate rooms, but I'm sure they are different spaces. I had a studio once and loved it. Now I have a bigger house, but it took me years to figure out this advice.

Write a quick list of all your current spaces. Bathroom, bedroom, living area, kitchen, etc. Just list all your spaces.

Now next to the space, write its current purpose. You might write "sleep" next to the bedroom, or "watch TV" next to the living room. Continue on until you have labeled the rooms for their current purpose.

Custom Shifting Cleaning and Organizing Company Presents: Home Energy

SPACE (ROOM):   *PURPOSE:*

You'll be surprised that I bet each space has definite room for growth. Most of the time when people start on their change journey, our spaces might not include the verbs we decided that make us happy. I did write watch TV on my living room list, because that's what most living rooms are for. I actually don't like watching TV and I can't sit still long enough to finish a show. But I had a whole room whose purpose was something I didn't enjoy? Cooking was not on my list and I had a huge kitchen for cooking. That doesn't mean I should get rid of my kitchen. But I did discover that I could set up a corner of my kitchen for my sewing machine.

Writing the purpose of our spaces, puts into perspective that we probably are not using our space to its full advantage. There is potential to possibly work your space to better serve the priorities on your list to make yourself happy. This definitely changes the way your home feels to you, and the energy of your space.

Chapter 7
The What and the Way

First of all Congratulations for establishing the balance between what you have now and what you want to change. The "What" is what you want, and the "Why" is why you want it. It could be you want a bigger floor space for yoga, or you want that reading nook because reading is your passion. Either way I hope you have a list now and a solid understanding of *what* and *why*. The hardest part of change sometimes is making the decision that you have to change something to begin with. Acknowledging that your space does not suit your passions and doesn't make you feel the way you want to feel is a huge step in the process of change.

The "How" is a formation of different strategies and processes that will accomplish your goals. Understanding the "How" is a very important step in completing tasks to get to the end result. The action part of the plan is the *How*. How can you get the "what", after you know why you want it. Making the choice to move forward toward your goals is the first step, and now you have a reason to do it.

I did it once, let my house "go", I just looked one day and realized my house was what I was. It became scattered, confused and unkept. My house mirrored myself at that time, and I realized that I wanted more. When I made that a priority, everything changed. The next few chapters focus on organizing, letting go and determining if what you have is really what you want. Read on and take notes if you can as you go. Knowing what you want is great, but actually getting what you want is even better. You can do this.

Remember that for some people, decisions are hard. It takes assertiveness, self-confidence and self-worth to make decisions easily. It is hard to trust ourselves enough to never regret.

Chapter 8
Organizing

It will definitely seem overwhelming to tackle everything all at once. That is why we don't. Do it a little at a time. Let's go over some basics, then break it down into actual accomplishable tasks.

By far the easiest way to organize anything is just to sort it out. Luckily it starts out that simple, making piles of similar things. The first step to organizing is by putting everything of the "like" together. Get baskets or boxes or even big ziploc bags if they fit. Start with one thing, let's say books for example. When all the books you own are in the same place, then it becomes easier to mentally see the volume of the item in relation to your space and needs.

Do you have 100 books? That is ok for now, it all starts with sorting. Are your socks all in the same place? Your nick nacks? If they are, you are one step ahead of the game. So many of us have things spread all over the house that is hard to tell how much of one item we actually have. Organizing needs to start with sorting, getting all of the same items in the same place. Then you can judge how much actual space you need to dedicate to that particular item.

The common household items that will need the focus of reorganization in most homes are: clothes, papers, bathroom supplies and kitchen supplies. It is hard to keep up with folding laundry too, and papers can add up quickly. If you have a basket or box set aside and have piled it up with mail, and other papers, don't be hard on yourself. Leave that basket and continue to put your papers in it. Start small, our to-do list is large already. When a basket is full, go through the basket then if it makes it easier. Get rid of what you don't want and establish a way to keep or file what you do. Some people can get rid of the unwanted papers immediately and file when it comes in. Other people have a hard time doing this, and that's ok. We all do life differently.

    A tip I do at home is using binders filled with page protectors in them. I have one for each kid so I can slide in artwork instead of letting those pile up. My kids come home with tons of papers from school. I use the same type of binders for my bills because I was horrible with papers. So I just slide the bill to the back of the page protector labeled "Electric" and each year has a binder. I used to have a filing cabinet, but it took up too much room in my house. Whatever works for your space. Bless the people who scan and file electronically. I am not tech savvy. Even though so many places go paperless now, the papers can still add up for some of us.

    If you have multiple people in the house, I used a system like this with everyone having their own dirty laundry basket which makes it so much easier to sort the clean load from the dryer. This task is left to the time management section and best when it is enjoyed. By far the easiest way to do laundry is to do it the second it's done. I'd probably see a lot of eye rolls on that one. If it does tend to pile up, try listening to audio books or music while you fold laundry to make it more enjoyable.

    Some things we organize without overthinking. I automatically put my daughter's clothes in her room, not her brothers.

Do you have spoons in every drawer of your kitchen or just one? Some things in our house are already organized by default. But if we think about it, isn't it so much easier to put the spoons away knowing exactly where they go? Because they have a dedicated place. Cleaning, picking up or resorting is much less of a task if it's just putting back in its dedicated space. It makes it so much harder to have a cluttered home if our objects have a "home" to go back to.

Organizing can be fun and decorative. Think outside the box to fit your style or personality and function of your lifestyle. If you charge your phones in the kitchen, placing a cookie jar on the counter to hold chargers makes it cute and functional. Is there a nice way to store your coffee? I have those storage cubes for toys. Nice baskets with legos in one, magna tiles in another. It actually multi-tasks as my TV stand because we are limited for space in that department. But baskets are so handy for anyone. Especially in the bathroom.

Not too many people probably store our shower towels in the living room. They are usually in the bathroom. Which makes us all natural organizers, and also we can be fancy designers too. I know few people that don't end up having an abundance of bathroom supplies. So start by sorting the items into baskets for each item, or boxes whatever you have. I have no closets in my old house, so I have to get creative sometimes. I actually hung two shower shelves from a towel rod on the wall above my shower for extra space to hold soap and shampoo.

After sorting everything alike in one space, it needs a "home" in your house. If you cannot come up with a "home" for those particular items, that is what is discussed in the decluttering chapter. The point of sorting is to discover if you have the space to house all the similar items and if you have too many, and why we have too many, which we will go into later.

Clothes. Do you have small rooms or no closets like I do? I'll share some tips. Baskets for underbed storage are so helpful if you have the space for that. If not, it is possible to raise the bed with raisers. I also take a hook, like those used for towels or curtain rods and screw to a stud no higher than I can reach. I buy a chain from a hardware department, the ones with the bigger links. Get about 2-3 feet of it. Hang the chain from the rod. Next put circle shower curtain rod hooks on every link in the chain. Now you can hang your clothes on hangers and put the hangers on the shower curtain rod hooks. If you put the hangers all in the same direction, you'll be able to rotate the whole line back and forth and it will stack nicely on the wall and take up a very limited space. Also, if you're using a dresser, please fold your laundry in a way that every item is visible. I can fit so many of my daughters' shirts stacked in a line instead of a pile and they actually get worn this way.

Store things where they will be used. Again, we don't keep our toothpaste in our cars, most of the time anyway. Where do you read? If it is in bed, keep the books in the bedroom. Like our kitchen spoons are in the kitchen. Everything in your own space should have its own space, like it actually belongs there. You dedicated the space there because you saw it as important and it deserved to be there. Don't worry now if you don't have the space to store all that you wanted to keep, we will go over that later. Try to keep the coffee next to the coffee maker, then the next step is to make sure it has a nice home to stay there, like a decorative container, jar or shelve.

I'm not saying you can't have a tissue box in every room or a bunch of throw pillows. I do not believe that everyone should be simplistic or have a plain house. Everyone *is* different, right? The point of this exercise is just realizing how much of each subject matter you have. Then deciding where in your space it makes sense to find it a home. Some things we store, like winter clothes in the summer. We should keep our jackets, but we should have a place to store them. Deciding where you will store it and how much space you have dedicated to that item, will make the process easier.

Custom Shifting Cleaning and Organizing Company Presents: Home Energy

List your rooms and what you store in them:

ROOM: *CONTENTS:*

This book is designed for you to fill in your answers to the questions, please do so. To get your answers and successful path, simply read and answer the questions in this workbook honestly and then reflect. There is no way to fail and so much to learn and gain. Eliminate Doubt from your mind. You will succeed at this, and I promise by the end of this course, you will have the tools to change more than just your environment. Your *change* can spiral a lifetime of happiness, not just in your home, but in your life. Accept yourself and together we can change every single "I can't" into "I did it".

Chapter 9
Prioritizing

Refer to the list you made for Step Two, you wrote down who you are and what you love to do most. Mine had music and art. So I definitely should prioritize making a space for all the containers of art supplies I sorted in the last chapter. Was sewing on your list or cooking? If cooking is on your list and you know you'll spend most of your time home in your kitchen, focus on the kitchen room first. If reading was on your list and you read in the bedroom, start with that space. If you really just like watching TV, and people do that at home to pass the time, focus on the living room. Maybe you rent a room, or have a studio, and that's fine too. You might just have to be a tad more creative on refining the space.

If reading is not on your list, and maybe you realize you have a hundred books. Put that on the top of your list for decluttering in the next chapter. I actually don't even like to cook and realized I had a kitchen full of cooking supplies. Prioritize making a "home" in your home for the supplies on your love to do list. Do you like to entertain? Maybe you need those thirty-five plates then.

For step three, ask yourself the "how" question. Maybe for example, make a space for art in a huge kitchen that is filled with cooking supplies I will never use. Who says I can't use those cabinets for something other than kitchen stuff? I can choose to store my playdough next to the kitchen table because it makes sense in my life to do so instead of saving the kitchen griddle I've used once in five years.

Now you know how much of one thing you have, you can prioritize your space according to what you actually like to do. I really like to tile and realized I had tile in every room of the house waiting to be installed. I was way better off gathering all my tile and putting it in a tucked away spot out of sight. I know where it is when I'm ready to use it, but organizing is about having the "like" in the same spot and making room for the things that belong. So now my tile has a home. And clearly I can see I do not need to impulse buy anymore because the space it belongs in now is almost out of room.

Go to your list and prioritize.

Do you work from home and need an office space? Maybe you need a spot in your bathroom dedicated to makeup. Then think, how much space for makeup do you need for that. Remember this is your space and should reflect you and what makes you happy. Maybe reposition a plant in your bedroom to make your reading nook. Whatever was on the list for your love-to-do, needs to prioritize the space. It's possible you were organizing your items, and sorted through twenty-five cups, and hate washing the sink full. They might be taking up valuable space you use for something on your list. I bet "having many different cups to drink from" was on no one's list in step two. Maybe board games or video games, but probably not having a ton of different cups. What if you can't do yoga because you have no floor space due to the furniture that is used as storage for other stuff. If so, is that stuff on your list of importance?

Think back to Step One now. The feeling you want to feel in your home. Do those extra cups you might have bring you the adjectives you described? Freedom, Acceptance, flexibility, safety, peace and fun. Those were my adjectives. Nah, the cups do not matter on that list. Sort your things, and then find a "home" for those particular items. If you realize you don't have enough physical storage or space to store them where you decided they belong, then it is time to declutter. Also, if it does not fit your priority list to make you happy, those items need to be decluttered too. It may sound hard, but we'll get through it.

Custom Shifting Cleaning and Organizing Company Presents: Home Energy

PRIORITIZING MY SPACE:

Chapter 10
Decluttering

Decluttering can be so rewarding even if it sounds big and scary. If you have already gone through your stuff and now have your piles organized, then we are ready to de-clutter. You've got your piles sorted in one space, your sewing materials, book, socks, etc. Now you can decide what is the least important and most important on your list judging by the verbs you wrote down on Step two.

Were there 25 drinking cups on your list in Step two? I am guessing probably not. If there wasn't, then those cups are just not making you happy. It is true, and you could use that space for something else. Prioritize your list to keep; by what you have rated the most important. If sewing is your happy place, hopefully you have put all your sewing materials in one place and separated the string and fabric into different boxes or containers. Step three is finding a place for what is truly important for having a happy space for you. This is where decluttering comes into play, letting go of what doesn't make you happy, to make space for what does. Most of us don't have a sewing room, but if we prioritize our hobbies, sewing *could* land a dedicated happy space in our home.

Refer to Step One every time as your guide.

With each object that is overflowing the space you have dedicated to each item, ask yourself if that object aligns with the adjectives you wrote for your space. Example is: will twenty blankets make me feel safe or give me freedom or create a fun environment. Safety, fun and freedom were on my list of what my home should feel like. Answering your own question of what you wanted to feel in your own space. If the excess items do not fit in with your adjectives or verbs, then those nouns can be passed along and donated to someone else who might have a different list. I do not need ten pans if I do not like to cook. Do those extra pans bring me fun? No, but they might to someone else. Every house is different because every person is different. Loving your space means it reflects you and that means you are being true to who you are.

What if you have the space for everything you sorted, and don't need to get rid of anything to make room for what you enjoy? That's great. Most of us have something we don't need and are willing to choose to let go for our happiness. .

Sometimes it is tricky to decide if our possessions are *"clutter."* Clutter is basically anything that does not have a "home". Again, your kitchen spoons have a home. Most of us have more than five spoons, that doesn't mean we can't have extra. Having extra is nice, but if we had so many that the drawer won't close, then the extra should go into the overflow pile. Furniture is a big one for many people, huge in fact. Some furniture we need for our space, and some is just taking up space. If I have a storage cube with nice baskets and every basket is filled with objects, it can't be clutter right? It can! This concept took me a while to learn myself so no judgment if you don't agree. The point is prioritizing your space to make yourself happy so there is no wrong or right way.

Shoving things into a dresser or closet to "hide" them, still means it is taking up space in our lives. For example, maybe that space would be better used as just space. It could be more floor space for my dancing or yoga. I used to think that as long as it was organized, it wasn't clutter. I did this process myself in the workbook. I sorted and laid out all the kids coloring books that were already nicely packed in baskets and realized I had fifty, most of which they had outgrown. Getting rid of most of them to a second hand store freed up enough space to eliminate the shelve that held those supplies. And we liked the open space. Art was on my list, but when I broke it down even more, I realized that coloring books were the last art project we'd ever do. And most certainly I didn't need that many.

This is the reason we sort before we let go. And prioritize before we sort. We already decided what was important, now we know we need a space where those activities can take place. So decluttering can be fun and rewarding if you keep in mind the end result. Of course some of our household items do not add up enough to have their own space in our house. That is why we all have "junk" drawers. Some of us need those junk drawers.

Remind yourself of your list: (put it on the fridge if you need to remember)
What I want to feel in my home
Who I want to be in my home
Why I think I am not getting that out of my home
What I need to make those goals come true
And what I do not need to make those goals happen

Try setting aside one group of objects, not on your happy list. Maybe that stack of random cords and plugins you forgot what they go to. Or those very outdated electronics that collect dust. Or those unused candles you swear you'll light one day.

The point of this exercise is to make a choice over what you chose as a priority for who you are and actually what you have and make sure it aligns. Collecting is easy, letting go is hard. It's not as hard if we have a reason in mind, a solution, a new adventure. Something we are passionate about.

Custom Shifting Cleaning and Organizing Company Presents: Home Energy

OBJECTS THAT DO NOT HOME A HOME IN OUR HOME:
(DOES NOT MEET UP WITH WHO WE WANT TO BE)
HOMELESS IN OUR HOME:

Chapter 11
Collecting vs Hoarding

I need to touch on this subject matter before we dive into letting go. You sorted your stuff and realized you might have fifty elephants scattered all over the house. I don't, but I wish I did. Is that hoarding? No, it's collecting. Here is where the line is crossed, ask yourself, do those trinkets have a "home" in my space? A place that is not in the way of accomplishing your hopes and dreams? Do you love to look at them or are you keeping them because you feel like you have to? Perhaps they were gifts you feel guilty about parting with. **Why am I collecting it?** Because, if it makes us happy, *why* does it make us happy? Maybe those objects bring us back to the adjectives in Step One? Peace, joy, comfort, belonging.

Collecting is just that, collecting. When we hold onto things just for the sake that we cannot or have not gotten rid of, then it's hoarding. I bet there's very few people in the world with excessive amounts of working microwaves on their kitchen counter. But a few of us might have broken ones in the garage that we know we need to get rid of. We don't collect some things because it makes no sense. We do collect pictures though, because why would we feel the need to get rid of them. Collections can make you happy, and hoarding, or not letting go, makes you weighed down.

Objects people tend to collect: gifts, antique dishes, trinkets, vases, glass objects, furniture, seasonal decor, clothes, cleaning products, jewelry, books, and toys, stuffed animals. It's perfectly fine and comforting to collect a theme or particular item. Just remind yourself those objects need to have a home in your home. They should not be taking up the space you could otherwise use to accomplish the verbs in Step Two. If your style is to have a collection, it's perfectly ok to do it, if it has a space in your house you can dedicate for just that collection. Boxes of clothes that don't fit anymore, but might fit someday is not a collection that makes you feel good. Realizing we are holding onto something for the wrong reasons, is the first step to letting go and shifting the energy that surrounds those objects.

A good example is Covid, everyones not so favorite subject. I'm not talking about the physical traits of Covid itself, but the mental, emotional and environmental changes that have occurred in the years during and after. Covid sparked a new generational change in the way we think about holding onto things physically. Driven by fear. Who would have thought that as a nation, we would ever see the day that we collected toilet paper? People hoarded toilet paper out of fear of not having any. The Covid era made it socially acceptable to hold on to things "just in case". A thought that we can never get it again and so must stock up and hold onto things as much as possible. Not use those items, but stockpile them. Holding onto something out of fear, is not collecting. Collecting something brings you joy. I think we can all agree that collecting animals is not a good idea, but collecting plants is perfectly okay.

How do I collect?

Do you keep those vases out of fear that you might have too many flowers and not enough vases? Or do you collect them because they make you happy? You feel good everytime you look at your vases. Or all they all just stacked in the back of a cabinet somewhere that you can't even see taking up space. If they are, they are something we feel we can't let go of. It's not a collection anymore, it is just taking up space in our lives. Collections can make you feel good. Hoarding is almost always being kept for the fear and anxiety of letting go.

The importance of home energy was definitely magnified during covid. We were all staying home more. Instead of our homes as an entertaining space, it emerged into a sanctuary. Our safe place, our happy place. So many people work from home now, more than I ever thought possible when I dreamed of the future as a child. This is the work from-home generation, people work, eat and sleep at home. There has never been a better time to turn your home into peace, safety and comfort. Your home should not bring you fear, anxiety or ill emotions. Nor should it be cluttered in the form of not being a functional space for you to thrive in.

Custom Shifting Cleaning and Organizing Company Presents: Home Energy

Clutter is what is not organized or sorted

Collecting is something you can visually see that brings you emotional joy or peace

Hoarding is holding onto because you don't let go

Pick one thing you "collect" and ask yourself these questions and repeat with each item:

Did I collect a... ? Or did you just decide not to let it go yet? (i.e. bunch of napkins)

Did I collect... ? Or just haven't donated them yet? I.e. coloring books)

Do we actually collect... ? Do we intend to use it someday? (i.e. clothes that don't fit)

We don't collect clothes that don't fit, napkins and coloring books. People collect things like dolls, spoons, nick nacks, antiques, gallswears, books, pictures, etc.

After you establish the difference between collecting and not letting go, then you can decide further if your collections have gotten out of hand at all. It is easy to do. I had collected too many art supplies for my space. I just didn't have the storage. But I prioritized, organized and let go of what did not fit in my space because I was holding onto them. Realizing that most things you can replace when you are ready to actually use them, makes it easier to let go.

Remember that if it is a collection, it should be put out where you can see and enjoy, if you have to store the items in hiding, it might not be something you actually want to keep, you might just not want to let it go.

Sometimes we don't even know why we want to keep it, we just cannot stand to give it up. Realizing those items are not on our happy list but they will make others lists, is the key to making that choice. It is a choice to let go and we all have to choose it for that to happen. This theory applies to all choices in life, if they don't serve our happiness, we can make new choices.

Custom Shifting Cleaning and Organizing Company Presents: Home Energy

Try making a list of objects that you have noticed you have multiples of and deciding whether you think it is a collection or you just have too many.

WHAT I COLLECT: WHY I COLLECT IT:

WHAT I HAVE TOO MUCH OF: WHY I HAVE TOO MUCH OF IT:

Chapter 12
Letting Go

Just the word "hoarding" has a negative vibe. It's actually not a great sounding word, I prefer to think of it as "holding onto", because that is exactly what it is. We hold onto something for some reason and choose not to let it go. Sometimes, we don't even realize we are doing it. We can add objects to our home little by little and then all of a sudden, we have too much.

This is a hard subject for some and others will pass with a breeze. Do not feel bad about yourself. I want to remind you that I have no interest in trying to turn everyone into a simplistic lifestyle. That works for some and for others, it is not our personality. My sister is very simple in her lifestyle. She gets rid of anything without attachment or fear. Her walls might seem bare, but that is her style. I am a recovering hoarder. Not the kind we see on TV shows, but I struggled with getting rid of anything. If it came into my home, it stayed. If you have ever wondered how you ended up with "this much stuff", I see you. I understand and we'll get through this.

It is hard to let go. Just in general, whether it be people, places or things, experiences or feelings... letting go is hard. We have to recognize, experience, process, and document then we can move on and let go. *It is a process*. Some of us can call out of work and not think about it the rest of the day. Some of us feel guilt, shame and anxiety about our choice and the feelings linger. Some of us have trouble making that decision at all. While letting go of an experience is different than material subjects, the process can be similar.

In both instances, we can feel like we are letting someone down, the boss, the coworker, the kids, but most importantly ourselves. I want you to think about how not letting go of something truly affects how we treat ourselves. You are letting yourself down by holding onto negative emotions or experiences. It is extra baggage to carry around emotionally, or mentally and takes up space that better energy could thrive. Holding onto physical baggage can take up the physical space that could otherwise offer a place of good energy as well.

Why do we hold onto things? Do any of these reasons ring true with your experience in not letting go? Please make a note to yourself if they do. You established the "what" of holding onto, this is the "why". The "when" comes with time.

Why people tend to hold on to things:
Sentimental value
Emotional reasons
Brings good memories
The fear of letting go
It might be useful one day
Had a plan to use it
It is still in good condition
Was given to us by someone
Fear of lack, or loss

Any other reasons you can think of? They are not *reasons*, they are *excuses*. But all of these reasons stem out of fear. We are afraid to let it go for some reason. We give those items the power to control our happiness. My little girl is a collector, but her collections get out of control to the point of not letting go. She collects stuffies. She has so many that I bought her a bunk bed to house them. They do have a space in her room. She never plays with them but cannot let them go, she feels the need to still desire more of them because they make her happy. But she has so many that she couldn't find an exact one and can't remember which ones she has. Her hoarding is filling a void. They do make her happy for a little bit, then they add to the pile and she can't part with them.

Fortunately for her and I, she will shortly outgrow her stuffie "collecting" with age. But the habit is similar, she is afraid to let go of them. She thinks she is collecting out of love, she loves those toys. She loves every one of them. So shouldn't she have them all? Unfortunately, she lost a lot of people in her life in the past few years, so she is afraid to let go of what she can control.

Every fall, before Christmas time, we go through our toys. Our family decides what to donate to others to make space for new stuff. We are grateful and lucky to have this option to change. My kids have no problem donating their things if they know they will help another child. My daughter can give away a stuffie thinking it will bring another kid joy and they will love it. This love cancels the fear. The fear of letting go is replaced by the happiness that someone else will love it. It is a beautiful thought and helps so much with the transition of letting go.

ARE WE HOLDING ON FOR LOVE OR FEAR?

Do we love having all those extra kitchen supplies? Or are we afraid that if we give it away, we will need it? It will come in handy someday. Someone gave us that for Christmas one year. People are way more important than things, they just are. And good mental memories are by far more valuable than the items they might be attached to.

I want to share my personal emotional struggle with letting go. A total irrational fear of loss that was *emotional*. When my Gram died, I inherited the contents of her house. It was a single wide manufactured home and her house was clean and kept. Everything had a place. I had no idea how many things, objects and materials she had fit into her home until I took them home via truck load. I had just bought a big house, and it was basically empty. Her things didn't take up my whole house like it did hers. But I didn't have a place for most of them, they did not have a "home" in my home. They either didn't fit my space or were not intended for my life. So much furniture to hold all of her items. It was overwhelming.

My Gram meant the world to me. So it was an honor to have her things, her energy. So many years went by and I gathered my own things. Pieces that I wanted at that time for my own space. I moved her things around countless times trying to find a place for them. I just couldn't let go. I felt guilty or sad, almost like I was losing her again. But I had more memories with her than with her stuff. It was just stuff and didn't contain her soul.

It was hard little by little to get rid of one piece of her furniture at a time. One thing I was sick of moving I had to let go, one at a time. It was a healing process. In the end, I honestly wish I could've gone to her house when she was alive and picked out just one item to keep. Inheriting all her things was overwhelming and a huge emotional burden she would have never placed on me. My sister would have been a better choice to have been in charge of the things because she can let go like no one I've ever seen. But it was me. And through that tough emotional process, I learned so much. I was forced to overcome those feelings of loss and guilt to let go.

I still have a few pieces of her things left. But they have an actual place in my house and serve a function. I will not hold onto material items again thinking the happiness they bring me outweighs the guilt and sadness. I kept those things out of fear, not love. I did love her so much, but her things are not her. Her memories can never be sold, given away or donated. They have a place in my mind and heart and belong there. I am reminded of her in so many ways, everytime I see a hummingbird, or use my sewing machine. I don't need her things to feel her love. And I am not afraid to let go anymore.

The reason I wrote this book is to help people, which is by far my favorite pastime. I always tell my kids to learn from my mistakes so they don't have to make them. You can learn from other people's mistakes just like you would your own without having to make them yourself. Saving you time and energy in the process. Energy is Energy. The energy it takes to clean your house can seem like a lot. But the energy to go through something emotionally or mentally can equal the physical energy in the body too. It can be a lot too.

We put an emotional value on things. Getting rid of a broken piece of furniture I got at a yard sale wouldn't not be as hard for me to have donated, but her stuff was hard. It wouldn't have mattered if the object was worth more financially or not. I threw out my sink cabinet that leaked and molded without question. We value our things emotionally most of the time over the cost. Then we are keeping it out of fear of letting go.

If we value something financially over emotionally, we fear that we won't have the resources in the future to replace it, so we hesitate to let go of that item. It is still the fear of letting go. In that case, it is just easier to sell a piece and justify getting the money, than to donate and feel we lost something emotionally in its place.

Ask yourself:
What value do I set on material things?

Are the ones emotionally valuable items harder to let go?

Why are they emotionally valuable to me?

And why am I afraid to let go of them?

What would I lose or gain if I let those items go?

Do I feel the need to replace that item?

Is it taking up emotional energy or physical energy?

Does that item actually bring me true happiness?

Now let's talk about how it might come in handy. This is a big one for most. Maybe we don't have extreme emotional energy into something but we fear if we get rid of it, we will need it someday. Sometimes this does happen. But letting go of the fear of needing it someday, will definitely free up space in your mind, energy and home.

When I was sorting my home, I did end up with a basket of random cords. Plug in and wires and who knows what. Now that they were all in one place, I decided to get rid of them all. A few months later, I inherited a tv without a plug in. I knew I threw one away recently, but I didn't regret that. I bought a new cord for seven dollars and moved on. Actually, ridding myself of the baggage that those random cords took up was freeing and I realized I could just replace the item later if I happened to need it.

Holding on to something because you might need it one day is like wearing a helmet every time you get in the car in case you get into an accident. It might happen, but being over prepared for it just in case is a waste of our energy. It most certainly means we are waiting and expecting for something bad to happen and almost look forward to it. We just can't and shouldn't live our lives like that.

You can and will get a different cord one day, and if you can't then you don't need it anyway. You will live without it. Letting go of the "just in case", or "what if's" is extremely freeing. What if I need that record player? You won't. What if I lose weight and those pants finally fit. You'll find new ones. We won't be as a nation walking around pantless anytime soon. Someone will have the pants you need. And the pants you have now that you're holding onto, someone is wishing you'd just donate so they wear.

Holding onto things we don't need does create a block in the system. Someone might be wishing for your kitchen griddle that you haven't used in years. It might be on their verb list of their favorite things to do. Pass it on. Feeling guilty about throwing a perfectly good item away is a large reason some of us can't let go. It works, it's useful. But not useful to us. Luckily there are so many places now that take donations and places online to donate. I prefer to just give the items I am willing to part with away. It's an energy exchange. I free myself and get space, and they get something they want by taking it off my hands.

I stopped collecting my items for a future yardsale that will never happen because I personally do not like hosting yard sales. I love the feeling that I might help someone with my item and that someone might appreciate it too.

Sometimes we know we don't want it. We set it aside. Like my attic, the land of no return. If it is not seasonal decorations, then once it goes up there, it stays. If I put something up there out of the way, what I am mentally saying is "I don't want this enough to give it a space in my home, but I don't want to get rid of it… yet." The extra storage space is a curse. If you plan on putting something away and it's not seasonal, you just don't want it. But I totally agree with this being the first step to parting with things. It's definitely a step in the right direction. Like I said, for those people who can put the unwanted stuff in their car and drop off to donate the second they don't want it, that's amazing.

For the people who have a hard time getting rid of things, putting them out of sight is a great first step. I started taking things out of the house, and putting them in the garage. Realizing how full my garage was, one day when I was ready, I got rid of the things I had piled in there. I was able to decide at that time, I was not going to use them and I didn't need them and they were taking up too much space in my life.

The value we put on objects has a lot to do with it. We may save our cans because they can be recycled or traded for money. We tend to wait until we have many bags of them before we get rid of them. We don't intend on keeping them forever though. We also don't have a hard time letting go of them because we cannot see a use for them. We do not fear being without them and we want to get rid of them. They have little emotional value in our lives. They are just cans.

We have all the power to let go. We take our trash out. We don't save some things because it has no emotional or financial value. Yet, we do pay to have our trash removed. Interesting thought. We put a value on how bad we want our trash removed, that we pay for it. We do this to declutter our space and up our energy. I don't want my trash. It has no value to keep, but a value to discard. Most of the things in your house can be donated for free though. So keep that in mind.

Not ready to say goodbye: Another big reason people hold on to things is because they didn't get a chance to let go to begin with. Imagine me just getting rid of all my daughter's stuffies without telling her and then she walks into the room, devastated, crying and upset. How would she feel? Betrayed, empty and lost. There would be no happiness in that separation. She wouldn't get a chance to properly go through the process of letting go physically so she can let go emotionally. Some people believe that just going through someone's home and getting rid of everything they don't need for them will solve the problem. This is not true and usually spirals the behavior of hoarding. They have to let go themselves.

Not going through the process of healing through recognizing emotions and letting go, is like stacking your emotions in your mental attic. One day you will have to come to terms with the mind clutter and assess the situation or it will clog up your space and energy. They are emotions we don't want to feel right now, that we have packed away, but they are still there and we have not let go. On the other hand, in a few years, my daughter will gladly be ready to donate the stuffies because she has outgrown them and will experience no loss emotionally. Being ready to face the feelings of letting go is an important step to change.

Was there a time in your life that you "stored" your emotions in the mental attic to forget and move on, but have not yet let go? If we are holding onto emotions we have not dealt with mentally, sometimes we hold onto physical objects to replace the need to let go. So we hold on to them. Interesting thought but so true.

Ask Yourself:

Was I ever forced to let go of something I was not ready to lose?

How did that loss feel?

Does holding onto something physical actually replace the feeling of the emotion of what you lost?

Do I feel good about holding on?

Can I let go emotionally of what I lost?

How would I feel if I let it go?

When I was teenager I moved out of my childhood house when I lived with my parents. They were moving and I couldn't take anything with me. I left it all behind, which in turn was disposed of. Very little items from my childhood I got to keep. I never got to properly say goodbye to these things I deemed as important at the time. Situations like this make it harder in the future to let go because we fear letting go. There was a negative feeling attached to the way we lost because we were not ready to lose it and didn't get to say goodbye properly.

If you have a hard time getting rid of "stuff", try having a proper goodbye for your items. Thank them for the experience and emotions they brought into your life and say goodbye. Wish that item good luck on their journey to touch others lives. If the item can't be saved, have a true goodbye. Some objects have reached the end of their "life", and so their material life in this world has ended. A couch that has completely fallen apart or a dresser that just can't be reused. The item will still continue its life. It will get recycled or even possibly restored by the right person, or maybe just renewed into the earth. It's ok to let it go. Appreciate it, then say goodbye and let go and move on. The loss of material things can feel like a death in our lives sometimes, so just be grateful that you had the time with the item to begin with, treasure the memory and let it go.

I might need this... Then there is the "I might need it" excuse. Of course we might need it. Some things we keep because they are functional, some things we keep because they have attachment to us or some we feel like we shouldn't get rid of. Some of our material things have a past place in our hearts, some have a future place in our mind. *Someday* we definitely plan on using that picture frame we have been storing for three years. Can't get rid of it because it has a future space in our home. Someday, we will get to that craft. Someday, those pants might fit. The issue with thinking this way is that it is still fear that is driving this not letting go feeling. It is being kept because we are afraid if we do not keep it now and store it, that when the time comes when we want it, we will not have it.

We try to predict our future disappointment by preventing the need to go without. Our future self probably won't miss that item at all. It is just a fear that might stem from our past. Maybe we do miss something from our past, but it probably isn't an item. It is possible it is a feeling or emotion that is missed instead. Maybe we miss feeling safe, abundant and free. Try not to worry so much about items you will need in the future. Life changes everyday and evolves. We evolve. Our needs and wants change, we change.

Think back to your first electronic, or your first musical device. Depending on your age, it's probably completely obsolete by now. There was no need to save tape decks from the 90s, even CDs are fading out. Technology changes just as fast as we do. When I was a teenager, no one had cell phones. I could never imagine that everyone would have one and we would not live without one. I did not see that coming so fast. It's pointless now to hold onto old iphones or tablets, they are outdated now in a matter of years. Holding onto material things for the future is hard to predict. Bread can't be saved for future generations to enjoy. What we can pass down is our knowledge. Our experiences, our lessons, our values. These are what are important to save and share and treasure.

Some things are easier to get rid of than others. The snowman that was created in the first snow, will eventually melt before it gets rebuilt. The snowman is built, we don't knock it down, we don't get rid of it, it just stays until it melts. We don't get too devastated by its disappearance because we know we can have something similar to it again. We are used to it coming and going and the fun of rebuilding. We appreciate and value it while we have it, but we let it go without severe emotional disturbance.

The things we hold onto can be looked at in the same manner. If you do decide to let go of something, we should trust in ourselves that we can get it again if we need it. The idea that it is not lost, or gone forever and can easily be replaced if we need it, adds comfort to the decision to let go.

Appreciate it while you have it, but understand its value lies in the memory of the emotion, not the item itself. So it is ok to let go. Try writing down the way that something you need to let go makes you feel. Take a picture of it so you can remember. It's so easy now to take pictures of everything with our phone. Keep the picture and journal what you want to remember. You don't need an item to remind you. You can remind yourself what you are afraid you might forget by writing it down. When you get rid of physically what you've been holding onto, you can still feel what you want to feel emotionally *without* that item, just by remembering. The mind and memory can hold so much more than any physical space can.

Someone gave it to us: Use your judgment here. If it's a smaller item of immense emotional value, I'm sure it makes you happy. You should definitely feel you can keep in your home objects that mean a lot to you. It adds to the good energy in your space.

I had someone in my life for quite some time who was an avid yardsaler. They would constantly go to pick up items for the kids and I, because shopping made them happy. I would end up with stacks of things this person gave me that I didn't necessarily want just because they gave them to me. I would feel guilty about immediately getting rid of the gifts because they frequently visited my home and I was afraid of hurting their feelings if they saw the items missing. What I had to realize is that shopping did make them happy. They were doing what made them happy. I accepted them and I didn't hurt their feelings.

It was also acceptable for me to make myself happy and set boundaries within my home and donate the items I didn't feel I wanted. Telling them not to bring them in the first place would've made more sense, but I was still proud of myself when I got to the point that I would pass them along without guilt. Also important to note that when you tell them you decided to not accept items you have no use for, that if they did not honor your decision, they are not respecting your boundaries. And boundaries are important to set and it allows others the chance to choose to respect you.

People give because they like to give. I love giving Christmas presents. I love giving to others. I don't necessarily do it for them, most of the time I do it for me. My kids would love me just the same if I cut the presents on Christmas in half. But it makes me feel good to give to others. Keep this in mind when someone gives you something, that they don't expect you to keep it forever. Some gifts are really sentimental and should be kept and valued, treasured and added to our "collections". However, if the reason you cannot let go of an item is because someone else gave you the item, it is not a reason to keep it.

Ask yourself:

What is something I can't seem to let go of?

How would I feel if I got rid of this? Is it guilt, shame..

What is stopping me from letting go?

Am I afraid of how they might feel or think?

Is that actually true?

Repeat this process with everything you cannot let go of

The truth is, is that someone who cares about us will not stop caring if we appreciate and move on. Obviously I'm not suggesting you refuse a gift from someone. Appreciate that they were thinking about you, enjoy that emotion, and when you are ready to let go of it physically, remind yourself that you still have the happy emotion from receiving it to begin with. Remember that old saying "it's the thought that counts"? Your thoughts and memories count more than the material item itself. And passing it along to others will also bring you happiness and spread good energy.

Guilt is a very powerful emotion that can be controlling in our minds and thoughts. Feeling free to make the choices we believe that are actually in our best interest comes from eliminating the guilt attached to those decisions. It takes practice. Every item might hold a memory for us. But after a lifetime of holding onto objects that contain a memory, eventually our space will be cluttered with no room for new "memories". Our memories should be stored mentally and not take up physical space in our environment. Our mind has the job of storing memories and we cannot be afraid to forget those memories. We will remember what we are supposed to remember as we change and grow through our lives and evolve.

Remind yourself you are letting go to make space for what makes you happy. You deserve to be happy and free. You deserve to love your space and have it reflect who you are and who you want to become. Everyone is unique and powerful and we have control over our environment.

I am a firm believer that mental health is just as important as physical health for your body. Negative feelings can weigh someone down the same as physical pain, and positive feelings can be just as rewarding as physical workouts. Energy is energy and it takes up space in your mind or body. The better we feel, the better the energy is.

Chapter 13
Bringing it back

Accomplishing the hard task of deciding to let go of some things in our home that we have held on, can be both hard and rewarding. Once you have made the decision to let go and release to make positive changes in your environment, the next step you can control is being selective about what you bring back into your space. You might have to revisit the organization and decluttering steps a few times on your journey. An important step is your to-do list and setting boundaries. Sticking to the "What" and "Whys" are a very important part of the process to getting to your desired results.

Custom Shifting Cleaning and Organizing Company Presents: Home Energy

Just to recap, ask yourself:

Have I decided who I want to be in my home?

How do I want to feel in my home?

What spaces are a priority?

What should I keep?

What should I donate?

How to set my space to reflect what I want?

I want to talk briefly about bringing things back into the home. Change happens all the time and that's the way it should be, it's ok to change your mind. Maybe you did love to sew but it bothers your back and so now you paint. Everything in the house should still have its own "home". A place it belongs and you return it when you are done. This keeps everything organized and decluttered. What we bring into the home is especially important for those that have accomplished the "hoarding" chapter. If you spend time or plan on spending time removing from your life the items that don't fit in, you should be especially careful when bringing new items into your space.

When you are out shopping and you see a piece you love, just *ask yourself "where in my space will I put it"?* Maybe you *do* have an empty wall it will go perfect on. If we just bring objects in without knowing where their "home" will be, they will end up lost, cluttered, or displaced. A simple trick could be planning on trading something you already have for something new you want. That keeps the balance in your home.

We are a sales driven society. We all like to save money. Most of us have a hard time passing up a good deal. We might buy something just because it is a great deal without knowing what we will do with it. For this reason alone, I have had to almost completely cut yard sales from my life. Some people can go buy something and it has a place, others might not buy anything except what they are looking for and some people buy whatever is a great deal. For years of my life, whatever came into my home, had a hard time leaving, so I now avoid bringing anything in. That depends on the person. No one should judge anyone for the way we are because we are all trying to be ourselves.

The point is, if it doesn't have a clear place in your home, then don't bring it into your home. That way you won't have to part with it later. It does not mean you can't shop, or collect. Just keep in mind your space. If you have a whole empty closet dedicated to christmas decorations because christmas decorating is your passion, and you see a christmas piece you can add and love, you get it. I don't have enough of that space and so many of us don't, but if the item has a home and you love it, then it makes sense to get it.

I have a toy room but it is small so before christmas, I have to donate some toys to make room for new ones. It is about accepting change and that is hard for some people. Think of it as a rug. Would you buy a new rug to put over your old rug? Then buy another new rug and keep stacking them? Or would you just trade out the rugs? No one needs a stack of rugs on the living room floor. Trading one thing for another is a good way to update your space and roll with changes. We all change everyday.

We usually wait until our current item needs to be replaced to replace it. We don't go buy a new microwave and set it next to our current working microwave waiting for the existing one to break. Maybe we collected fifty shirts and the older shirts can't be parted with, and that new shirt is just a good deal. Remember that if you had that empty dresser waiting for more clothes, this is not an issue. But if your current dresser is bursting at the seams and you already don't wear half the clothes you have, perhaps bringing more in the home isn't in your favor. Decide if you can trade an item, maybe your style changed or your body type.

Change is good. Being able to trade out things in your space for new ones, it is a great way to feel renewed. This takes practice for some people so be kind to yourself in your journey.

Just remember that everything in your home now should have a home of their own, their own space. So, if the item you want to bring into your home does have a place to go or does not fit in the junk drawer and will end up homeless, do not bring it home. I can't bring home every stray cat but I can appreciate the beauty of the lives I run into along the way.

Do you tend to bring home what you do not need, and then don't replace an old item with the new? That means we are not letting go of our past for some reason.

Ask Yourself:
Am I bringing in because I want change, if so that should be a replacement

Am I bringing in to fill a void?

What is the feeling I am trying to mimic and why do I think this item will bring that feeling?

Is this item the only way I'll ever feel that emotion?

How can I get that desired feeling without bringing in that item?

Chapter 14
Reasons we Don't do it

So many of us want change and we plan on doing it. There are excuses that we don't, not reasons. There is a difference between *reasons* and *excuses*. A reason makes it factual. An excuse tends to point the blame. "I have to work today". Is that a reason or excuse? We are choosing to work.. Some things, like the weather, are out of our control. Other circumstances, such as work, is a choice. We actually choose a lot in our lives, so those choices become our reasons. They can only become excuses if you blame them.

If you blame the boss for asking you to come in, that is our excuse. We are still choosing to go to work even if we feel forced. Being late for an appointment because your car didn't start is a reason. It is a fact. Out of our control sometimes. Please don't blame yourself for making excuses why you don't do what you plan on doing. Making a choice to make your to-do list a priority is the first step to accomplishing what you intend on doing.

Here are some of our "reasons" we haven't gotten to our space like we'd planned on:

Time
Energy
Other to-do lists take priority
Motivation
Low enthusiasm
Holding the mental space to do it

When we look at this list, we realize that these "reasons" might be choices. They are choices, but are we blaming them on something else? So actually they are not reasons, but excuses. Let me explain.

A reason someone can't vacuum might be they have a physical ailment that makes it dangerous to do so. A person in a wheelchair does not have an excuse they can't walk. It is not a choice. That is the reason. Your time *is* actually your choice. It is. How you use your energy is your choice. Your priority list is your choice. How motivated or enthusiastic you are about something is something you can change and choose. And letting go and making the choice to change is also something you can choose to do. So we can overcome our excuses with choice. If you don't blame yourself, others or another situation, we realize our reason can be changed from "I don't have time..", to "I'm making the time".

"I don't have a closet". That's the reason. That is the reason I can't store a bunch of extra clothes in the bedroom.

"My landlord won't allow dogs". That's the reason you can't have a pet in your space right now.

"I can't seem to organize my things". Yes you can. You got this! Choose one thing at a time and encourage yourself through self motivation and the end result. That is an excuse where you are blaming yourself.

Just realizing that you have the power to choose and act will mean you have the control over your choices and space. It is hard not to look at excuses as reasons. But remember, excuses are blame oriented. "My kids make too much of a mess." Yes they do, it is my excuse. The reason they make a mess is probably they are not being directed into more of a controlled activity. Like they take out playdough and pick it up before moving onto the next project. If I just blame them with an excuse for the mess, it solves nothing. So how can we turn those "I can'ts" into "I did it!"?

Time is the biggest one. Time can be the biggest excuse. Everyone is so busy these days. We are handling the world and running all the time. I feel super proud that you put yourself and your space on your priority list high enough to read and engage with this book. You did it! You made the time for change. So it is definitely possible, it is tricky to balance but possible. Making time for everything seems impossible at times.

That is where the priority list comes in handy. I bet we'd all pay our electric bill if we had money in the bank and an electrical shut off notice. Electrictricity is a priority in our lives. We would make time for the call to pay the bill if we wanted to. If we had a flat tire, it would definitely be a priority to get it fixed. It depends on how bad you want the change to make it happen. Time is such a big issue, that there is actually a chapter on it. Please read it and take note. As time has been my personal excuse my whole life. I was meaning to write this book long before I did, because I kept the excuse that I did not have time. I decided to make it a priority in my life.

We can't make time, but we can save some time.

We can't go back in time, but we can choose how to use it. Everyday we each have the same number of hours in our day, we get to choose how to use them. Even if it feels like we do not have a choice. We are actually choosing how to use our time.

Energy. How can we find the energy? If the task seems overwhelming to accomplish everything at once, please just do one thing at a time. Start with organizing *one* thing. Go through one drawer, and make that a priority. The motivation will bring you energy if it is something you are happy about doing. Take the "I have to.." out of it and replace it with "I want to...". It will make the effort seem effortless if you enjoy it.

We use "I Have to" way too much in life. Examples:

"I have to take a shower;"
"I have to go to work"
"I have to watch my kids"
"I have to call..."

No. We are actually choosing to do these things. Try replacing "have to" with "want to".

"I want to take a shower"
"I want to go to work"
"I want to watch my kids"
"I want to call..."

Now we realize, these are choices. It makes what we choose to do our choice, and less of a burden in life. In reality, we are choosing these things. "It is one o'clock!" Is that a choice? No, we can't choose that, it is simply one o'clock. It is a fact statement. But there are a million other choices we can make and changes we can decide to be in control of our own lives. We should celebrate our freedom as individuals and be grateful for our different choices.

We choose our priority list. Say we really need to go to the bathroom. Again, it is still a choice to go to the restroom. How many of us would go get water and choose to sit and drink more instead of going to relieve ourselves first? I can bet the priority would be going to the bathroom first if we really felt the urge to go. Sometimes, other things on our to-do list get bumped to priority and then what we want to do, is actually last. That makes it feel like we have no time to do what we want to do. So we tell ourselves that we don't have time to do it. And that is our excuse. That we just have too many other tasks to do.

Did I choose to put it last on the priority list, so it is an excuse.

I choose to put that last.

Why did I?

Am I just not important enough?

Is your space not important enough?

Should I be happy and free and peaceful in my own home?

It is a priority and you have told yourself that. And change is on its way!

The exercise here to practice is: being the reason we are making choices, not the excuses we don't in life.

Chapter 15
Procrastinating

Remember those excuses? Procrastination goes hand in hand with it.

Procrastinating is bumping it down on the priority list. It's that simple. Your intended task was going to be first on the list, then something better came along, and it got bumped down. Then it got bumped down again, then we ran out of time, energy, or motivation. So now that task has to wait. Maybe it will get bumped back up to number one on the priority list again. And it is our job to keep it number one if we want to actually cross it off the list this time. There is no doubt the relief we get from crossing off our to-do lists. It's like a weight lifted off our shoulders.

How many times have you had the recurring thought that you should do a particular task? Every single time you look at the carpet and think "I should vacuum it". Or walking by a broken piece of furniture and thinking "I should get rid of that". Some people can do that right then and there and that's awesome. It takes practice for most of us, so don't be hard on yourself. I am a work in progress in this area. What I can promise is the relief that comes from accomplishing something you were meaning to do, certainly has its weight in gold.

Every time we think about something and don't do it, it takes energy in our bodies. We keep thinking about it and can't let it go. As soon as it is crossed off the list, it is gone. Keep in mind this only works for good energy experiences. If you think about punching someone in the face, and you do it, that decision will affect you for a long time. Do only what brings you no guilt or no shame. That which brings positivity and good energy into your home and life. You can experience great joy by doing what you think about, as long as it is a positive choice. You are worth it to make changes, so put yourself and your energy up on your priority list.

If something has been bothering and bugging you or nagging on your mind, it will create a dragged down feeling in your body. This is also about letting go and trusting yourself. Have you been thinking for a while about calling someone and don't? Some tasks are easier to bump down on the priority list. If we run out of cat food and have hungry cats, we probably make that higher on the list. If you cut your finger and need stitches, I'm sure you would choose the hospital over moving that piece of furniture you wanted to move. That's not really procrastinating, that is more choosing the best course of action for your situation. The point is to make your home and space a priority, you have to make it a priority.

I can promise that accomplishing shifts energy. You will feel a weight lifting off your body and mind when you cross off your list of what you "have to", or choose to do. I am choosing to wash my dishes, and it's done. I am choosing to search and apply for that new job. If you have the thought about doing something over and over, please answer these questions:

Custom Shifting Cleaning and Organizing Company Presents: Home Energy

Think of a recurring positive thought that comes into your mind over and over about an action you think you should be doing:

Is what I'm thinking about a good choice?

Can I do what I am thinking about?

When can I make the time, energy and motivation to do this?

Will I feel better once I do it?

What do I need to do to make this happen?

I say positive thought meaning something that will not hurt yourself or others, usually the positive action thoughts will benefit us for the better. For years I kept thinking, I should write this book, over and over I thought about it. Most of the time the answer is just making it a priority and using time management skills to accomplish your goals. Shift the energy in your life.

Believing that you can do it starts with changing the "I will", to "I am".

Chapter 16
Time Management

Are you a list writer? Some people use "to-do" lists to keep their tasks on track. This is a good way of reminding yourself what you would like to accomplish within a timeframe. Whatever works for you. I like to-do lists because it takes the pressure of my brain to remember everything I need to do. Also, I feel a sense of accomplishment when these tasks get crossed off. I like to write a list for the day if I have time set aside to fit in anything extra. I write one for the week and the month and I love writing them for the future.

The to-do lists I write in advance for the future are my goals. What I know will bring me closer to my results I am striving for once I finish them. Having goals in mind makes you feel like you have something to work for and you are getting somewhere different. It eliminates the feeling of behaving like a gerbil on a hamster wheel. Going round and round and not getting anywhere. Even if your daily list is small, it is still an accomplishment and keeps us on track.

Please try this exercise:

Try for just one day to write down in a list of literally every single thing you do. From getting dressed, brushing your teeth, starting your car, eating lunch, etc. Just one day, write everything down you did. You'll need an extra page, I'm sure.

You will surprise yourself how many tasks you complete every day without thinking about if you have the time to do it. You will be shocked to see much you actually accomplish in one day. We know without writing into our daily schedule how long it takes to brush our teeth. We do it so much, it just becomes part of our day without the need to add it to our to-do list.

Custom Shifting Cleaning and Organizing Company Presents: Home Energy

WHAT I DO IN A DAY:

Our to-do list usually consists of tasks we are trying to squeeze into our day. Extra things we are trying to accomplish. Something we are solving or fixing or adding to our day to avoid a negative consequence. We need to get groceries once a week, pay bills, make appointments, or phone calls, check our mail and our email and respond. Sometimes we do everything on our day off, once a week or once a month. Sometimes we try to squeeze in our tasks into our already busy day.

Some of our tasks don't have a set place on our to-do list or a spot at all and we do them whenever we can. We run out of clean socks, so we do the laundry. Our dishes pile up, so we wash them. We ran out of fruits and veggies, so we went to the store. It actually makes time more stressful if our tasks have no set place. Like our material items in the home not having a set place. It's clutter, mind clutter. Think of non-delegated tasks in our day, week or month as time clutter.

We can feel stressed that we didn't have the time set aside to fold those five loads of laundry. It doesn't have a time "home" like brushing our teeth does. Because it is not in our daily routine, it can now get bumped down our priority list and procrastinated.

Custom Shifting Cleaning and Organizing Company Presents: Home Energy

ROUTINES IN OUR LIFE:

        DAILY: WEEKLY:

Tasks out of my regular routine:

My motto is "Control What You Can". Our to-do list is something we can control. When we make a to-do list for the day, it doesn't include brushing our teeth. We don't need to write it down to do it, but we do it anyway. The tasks we write down on the list are tasks that might otherwise be forgotten or not put on priority. I write things like "pay the electric bill", because I know it has to be done and I don't do it everyday. A giant list everyday might seem overwhelming, so I try to keep it small unless I have the day off or a chunk of time set aside.

Besides knowing what needs to be done, the next step to managing your time is knowing how long each task takes. Paying my electric bill takes me about ten minutes. So I'll need to carve out a slot of ten minutes to cross off that task. Because I clean other people's houses for a living, I know how long it takes me to fold six loads of laundry. I have the exact time it will take me to complete the job. Not everyone knows this. If you have no idea how long it will take you to fold your laundry, time yourself next time you do it. Then you'll know when "fold laundry" is on your to-do list, how long you need to set aside for the task.

I strongly advise finding a fun way of doing something you don't typically want to do, but choose to do anyway. So definitely my advice if possible is listening to music or an audio book doing your laundry. You might look forward to that time instead of dreading it. I don't have a dishwasher, and I have a giant sink. I know it will take about three songs to do my dishes. I often pick these three songs and play them while I do my dishes so it makes the task more enjoyable. Really, it gives me the time carved out in my day to listen to three of my favorite songs.

Think about driving to work, if you do so. You notice your gas tank is nearly empty and you've got thirty miles to drive. Would you be able to say "I don't have time to get gas", and make it to work anyway? No, you'd probably run out of gas on the interstate if you procrastinated this task. Like was mentioned before, you'd get the gas and change the outcome of what could've been, even if it meant you might be two minutes late for work.

We don't always know how long it would take to get gas on a particular day. We can estimate, but it depends on other factors. Still, that task is bumped to priority because of its need. We cannot drive to work without gas in our cars, unless you go electric and still you need to charge up. Life works the same way. Sometimes, some things just have to be done to function properly, like sleep. We need to sleep. Sleeping hours are not doing hours.

Time management is about setting your priorities for your tasks, knowing how long the task might take, and setting a time to complete the task. It takes practice. The more you practice it, the easier it gets and the faster you get at accomplishing your list. We always fit in brushing our teeth. We make time to go to the bathroom without setting a stop watch. We can train ourselves to fit other tasks into our day as well without even realizing we are doing it. Especially if we decide what we are doing in our day is a choice, not a "have to". That mentality eliminates the "task" label altogether.

I choose to drink coffee in the morning. I might multitask by drinking my coffee while I get the kids lunches ready for the day. But I don't add "drink coffee" to my to do list. I just do it because I choose to do it, I made a personal habit with my morning coffee and it's my routine. Coffee in the morning makes me happy. If I wanted to sit and enjoy my coffee while looking out the window, I would actually just have to get up earlier to do that. And that would be my choice.

What if we just got our gas when we had half a tank left because we had plenty of time that day, and there was an empty gas pump? It is a better use of our time management and takes practice to cross things off the list before they even hit our list to begin with. Most of us get into routines. Routines are the easiest way to complete tasks without a list.

I know how long my morning routine takes. I feed the cats, let the dog out, make coffee, go to the bathroom, make lunches and snacks, get the backpacks ready, make sure my kids have their clothes set out, check the dogs water and food, while drinking my coffee and all before I get myself ready for the day. I set my alarm in the morning to accommodate my daily routine. Once in a while, I miss that alarm for whatever reason, then I have a choice. I choose not to skip anything on the morning list, so I can either do the routine faster or be late. I know from experience that I can do it faster, but it's not ideal and pretty stressful to do so. But it can be done and I would choose to do it faster over being late because being late makes me nervous and honestly that does ruin my energy.

I have practiced both routines and I choose to have enough time without feeling over rushed, so I know not to hit the snooze button in the morning out of experience. I don't like the feeling of being late, so I try to manage my time into a morning routine that fits my schedule. If I'm running late because something happened outside of my routine, like oversleeping or my dog escaping the yard, I can cut out of my routine what I can to avoid being late. Again, this is a choice. There have been mornings that I'm washing my face in my kitchen sink instead of taking a shower to cut out that extra 10 minutes.

I won't send my kids to school without lunch, so my shower gets bumped off my priority list, but in the end, I can still be on time if I choose to. The key is knowing how long something takes. Just from practice and experience. And making sure we set that time aside for the priorities. Sure, I could delegate my kids to make their own lunches. But a four year old might pack oreos, so I choose to get ready in a different way. Everyone's routine is different.

Custom Shifting Cleaning and Organizing Company Presents: Home Energy

Please answer the following questions using your notebook, or this book:

Do I have routines in my day?

Is there a morning or night routine that I use to make my day habitual?

My morning routine in rank of priority:

My night routine in rank of priority:

Do I know how long my routines take to complete?

Is there any room in my routine to add one accomplishment and still run smoothly?

Can I multitask any of my tasks without feeling overwhelmed?

When in my day do I feel rushed?

Maybe you realize your morning routine is already bursting at the seams, and you feel rushed and stressed in the morning trying to accomplish your to-do list. Realizing that, could shift the priority to set a different time to do some of these tasks. Maybe you might want to add taking your shower to your night routine instead.

Routines help us stay on track and become accomplishments that we don't usually notice as successors unless we write them all down and give ourselves credit for it. We choose to do tasks to avert the negative feelings we would feel if we otherwise avoided those. Not brushing my teeth in the morning would actually ruin my vibe all day, so I chose it. I have that two minutes because it is a priority to me.

I am a recovering time hater. I spent 40 years of my life cursing time with phases like "I don't have time." Or, "I have no time." I looked at time like a curse, not a gift. That way of thinking will surely stress anyone out. I took energy classes and in one particular class, we were learning breathwork. I skipped all the breathwork classes because I thought I didn't have time to breathe. That was a turning point for me. I didn't have time to breathe. That sounds ridiculous. I was looking at time like it was my enemy. Even saying things like "time is not my friend." If you are reading this, or listening to this, you are alive. So you have time.

It is up to us as each individual how we use our time. Time is a gift. Every second of every day is a gift. We can choose how we spend it and we can enjoy the choices we make. We can feel good about our decisions and value what we are choosing to do instead of dread and regret it. We have that freedom of positive thought, and our relationship with time is important. If you're like I used to be, cursing time for existing, it is hard to feel accomplished enough. It makes feeling successful hard if you feel "your time" is never enough to satisfy yourself. If you go through your day constantly feeling you are running out of time, you are not enjoying the gift.

Time is a gift and how we spend our time is our choice. Time is our friend and not our enemy. I know how hard it is to feel and think "there is no time for that", "I don't have enough time to do that". In this generation, an adult has a lot to accomplish. There is a lot of pressure to do everything to feel accomplished. We hardly ever think about what we already do that is amazing. We strive for what we "have to do" to feel a sense of achievement. We make big to do lists, and do not count our daily routines as success.

We do not give ourselves enough credit for what we already do, and blame ourselves if we fall short. We have the freedom to make choices in our time that give us the sense of accomplishment and we deserve to feel our energy was worth our time. We deserve to feel happy mentally, physically and in our own environment. And we have the power to change this if we want.

The habit to break here is not saying "I don't have time". We do have time, time is right now. It's the choice on how we use our time and that is the truth. Instead of believing you have no time for something, tell yourself you are choosing to use your time for something else. I did choose my chores over my breathwork. I did that. It wasn't that I didn't have time for breath work, I just chose other things on my priority list instead.

Knowing that how you use your time is a choice, eliminates the blame on time. It is not Time's fault if you choose to use it differently than you'd like. When I have trouble making a decision, my wise sister tells me, "do what brings you less stress." It helps me realize that no matter what decision I am making, it is my choice to do so. I can call out of work, maybe I would lose my job, but it is still my choice. Blaming others for our decisions has become all too easy. We might say things like, "I have to go to work". But honestly, it is our choice to go. We are choosing to pay our bills, and that should make us feel proud, not resentful.

Adults have more choices now in this generation than ever. If we feel trapped in our time, it is because we chose it. I chose to care for my children. I am a single Mom. It does require a lot of time and energy, but they are high on my priority list because I chose that. Blaming them for my time would be a total waste of my energy because it is my choice to choose them. My priorities are my children right now, and I look at that like a gift. I am proud that I am able to care for them. I am honored that I have that choice. We all have something to feel grateful for.

Our completed tasks are our ability to accomplish. You are capable of achievement. Even brushing my daughters hair is a choice and a success when I complete it. It is worth the effort and I choose to make the time to get it done.

My advice is to keep the "extra" tasks on your daily to do lists small, because you already have some daily routine that you use your time for. Start by writing one for the week, then break it up into smaller ones for the day. I know I need to renew my drivers license. It does not need to be done today, but by the end of the month. It is on the list, and I'll feel better energy when it is off my list, but I can prioritize other tasks around it. Not necessarily procrastinating my renewal, but choosing to do other tasks first because I know my renewal will take fifteen minutes online and can be done any time of the day. So today, I need to go to the bank when it is open.

My list is smaller now so I don't feel overwhelmed. Go to the bank, make a dentist appointment. I can fit that in my day. The key is when you cross something off your list, feel good about it. Feel proud and feel accomplished. If you don't have days set aside to go through your house and get rid of clutter or organize, don't get discouraged. Start small. One drawer at a time. Then when you do it, feel good about it. Never tell yourself "I have to do that," instead think "I want to do this and I'm choosing to do this". Then feel proud and accomplished when you cross it off your list.

It helps to think of the end result when doing a task. Just like working a job is worth it, if we think we will get paid. The payoff is a similar drive, the weight lifted off your shoulders is your reward when accomplishing.

Cleaning my fish tank is on my to do list. It is on my list because it is not in my daily routine, so it's on my "extra" list. I imagine how great the tank will look when I am done, and then get excited at how good I will feel when I accomplish it. The end result is my motivation instead of dredging the time it will take to complete it. The clean tank will make the fish happy and I will enjoy the sight of them happily swimming around. I won't have to look at that tank and think "I have to clean that soon". I'll just choose to clean it and feel good about it. I know cleaning it the way I'd like it to be done will take about a half hour. So I know I get that task done on the day I get out of work early. That half hour is so well spent because I won't spend the week thinking I need to do it everytime I look at the tank. I'll look at the tank all week after I do it and think "it looks great". That task will not be cluttering my mind.

Time management is exercised more efficiently when we know to prioritize our tasks, and we know how long that task takes and we choose to set the time aside for that task. When we practice choosing to fit accomplishments into our schedule, we can eliminate the feeling of procrastinating. Choosing something without dread helps us to feel successful without animosity.

In one of the classes I took, the instructor asked me a simple question. If I could be anything I wanted to be or do for a living without restriction, what would that be? That was easy. I'd be a writer. Then I asked myself why I wasn't a writer and if I thought I could not be a writer... Was it because I didn't think I had time to write a book? I'd even written on my to do list to write this book. Even if none of my books sold, I would still be a writer if I wrote it, right?

Why did I convince myself for so many years I didn't have time to do something I wanted to do? I put the priorities on everything else and procrastinated what I wanted to do by lying to myself that there was no time for that. I'm sure I did it to protect myself out of fear. The truth is, I control my own time. So I could use my time to write a book if I choose to. Putting this book on my priority list, made it possible for me to accomplish what I wanted. I no longer told myself it wasn't possible. I just had the time somehow, by simply making it a priority.

We can all choose the time for what is the priority in our lives. We make our own to do lists. We can cross off whatever we choose to accomplish as long as we choose to make it a priority in our lives. This is a very powerful notion that we make truth into our daily lives. We can all change what we can if we believe we have control over our own lives. None of us are puppets. And if we choose what we want to accomplish, we will find a way to make that a priority.

If you find happiness in the accomplishment, that task will not be something you "have to do", but what you choose to do.

Thinking this way will turn your "to-do" list into a success list. You will feel the power you have to change and control your own environment in the way you choose to use your time.

Time is a gift and feeling grateful to have the ability to accomplish things, even the "chores" is a gift. We are lucky we can still do our dishes. Lucky to have laundry to fold. And I am so lucky I have children to care for. There is no point in wasting our energy with animosity going through tasks we choose to do and labeling them as "have to" chores. No one has to do anything. The only thing that is certain in life is death. You are not dead yet, so you have time. And how you choose to use your time is your choice.

I want to share with you a lesson I learned on time management. I had a dear friend who was having her 60th birthday party on Saturday night, but I waitress on Saturday nights. I told her "I had to work". The truth is, I should've told myself, "I want to work". Which would have sounded silly considering why I would choose work over her milestone birthday party. I blamed in my mind the fear that I might get fired if I didn't go to work. Or that I "needed the money", and "couldn't take the day off". If I had put her birthday party on the top of my priority list, I would have made sure I made the choice to attend her party. I had to learn to forgive myself for that choice and take it as a valuable lesson in time management. Time management means how we manage our time. How we *choose* to use our time. I made that choice, and unfortunately, she died a few months later and the memories I would have made at her party with her would have been priceless.

If we start now by replacing "I have to"' with "I choose to", our decisions will be easier to prioritize. When my daughter asks me to play with dolls with her, and I say, "I have to do the dishes", it really means, "I am choosing my dishes over play time right now." It is a hard pill to swallow sometimes, but it is the truth. Looking at our decisions like this, puts our to-do list into perspective. Using the excuse that we have no time, is not actually the truth. We are choosing to use our time in a different way.

Custom Shifting Cleaning and Organizing Company Presents: Home Energy

Please answer these questions for yourself:
Why do I choose to use time the way I do?

How is my priority list decided and why am I choosing what is on the top of the priority list?

Is that choice a priority out of fear or joy or truly a priority?

A real priority that can not be procrastinated is getting medical assistance for an emergency. Those decisions are the easiest to prioritize. It's still a choice, but usually a choice we don't think twice about. A lot of our choices we do because we feel obligated to, but remember that is still a choice to do it.

Chapter 17
Responsibilities and Obligations

Let's figure out where you stand with your plate. You know that saying "too much on my plate." Responsibilities are somewhat different from obligations. While both can be commitments, Obligations don't change and shouldn't be procrastinated. All obligations are also your responsibilities, but you are not obligated for all your responsibilities if your priorities change. Allow me to explain by making a list of my Obligations as you do the same for yourself. These are the wide views. There is no need to itemize each task included in each obligation. Feeding the dog lies under my pets.

My Obligations::
My 3 kids
My Pets: 3 cats, dog, fish
My house
Myself

Do not forget to include yourself on your list. For the rest of your life, you are responsible, *and* you have an obligation for caring for yourself. *Obligations don't change.* I have an obligation to my pets until the end of their life and the same goes for my kids. That is my view. There are a great ton of tasks that go along with being responsible for my house. But because I am a single parent, the home is all my responsibility, so I am obligated to make sure my children have a home. Everyone will have a different list, but every list will include "myself" and even partial responsibility of the homestead.

Responsibilities are what we have personally committed to. This list can change as our life changes. We decide what is a responsibility and commit to making sure that we are responsible for following through. Usually our responsibilities reflect our obligations.

My Responsibilities are:

My 3 jobs

School/Education

Building my business

Myself

No matter what our list says, I have chosen to believe that they are my choice, and I choose the responsibility and obligation of commitment. Work is my responsibility, but that's because I choose the obligation of my house, pets and kids, and my work provides for them. I can skip bath night for my kids one night, and still take good care of them. But I can't skip paying the electric bill and still provide a safe home for my family. So work is my responsibility that allows me to succeed at my obligations. I do need money to buy cat food, but I choose my cats.

I am not obligated to clean other peoples' homes, but I own that responsibility when I choose to do it for my job. When my child is sick and I choose to stay home with them, I then move care-taking to my priority list, and work gets bumped down. So I am not obligated to work then because I have obligations for my children as they hold the highest priority in my life.

This comes down to boundaries. This is a hard one for many. I struggled for years with boundaries. You actually are not obligated to answer the phone for the fifth time in one day for that friend who wants to complain. Not on the priority list. The reason is because that commitment does not work towards your responsibility list. If the commitment doesn't help with your responsibility list, it isn't a priority. Remember that YOU are on the responsibility list. Setting boundaries is crucial for time management and happiness. We can't "make" time, but we can find time. Letting go of what doesn't aid in our priorities, can free up time and energy for us to focus on what is important to us.

If going out with a friend for a late night encounter will make you too tired to accomplish your next day's commitments, it is okay to set boundaries and kindly decline without guilt. You are not responsible for others' happiness. Practicing self care is super important. I understand how hard setting boundaries can be. I recently turned down what seems like a great work opportunity because it would strongly affect the time I had for my kids. I had to look at my responsibility list and prioritize. While the extra money would have been nice, I would have forfeited the time and space I had to keep my own house. I am the one obligated for the care of my own house. I set those boundaries.

We all live somewhere, and we are all at least partially obligated for our living situation. Our space is a priority. Having electricity and water and somewhat regulated temperature should be a priority. Having food, water, clothes and a clean space to live helps us survive. It is part of taking care of ourselves. And we have a responsibility for life to take care of ourselves. Life is a gift, not a curse. The responsibility of taking care of ourselves is something we should value and treasure, not dred and procrastinate.

What you choose to put on "your plate" is a choice. But even without children and pets on the list, you will always have yourself as an obligation. And of course, I believe our personal space, our home, should be on the list. Everyone should have a roof over their head. And those of us that are lucky enough to call a house a home, should take pride in that responsibility. I should love taking care of my kids and my pets, and of course my home. Without the responsibility of it, I wouldn't have the choice to have them. Responsibility is power, it is choices, it is a gift. I am lucky to have a space to raise my children. We are all lucky to have a space to live and we can love our space if we are grateful enough to value it and choose the responsibility that comes along with the freedom of choices.

Obligations can easily be cursed when something goes wrong. Our plumbing goes haywire and it is stressful. If our dog needs immediate vet service, or our kid is out of school for a week with a sickness. One secret to help with the stress is gratitude. If we didn't have that toilet, we would never have a problem with the plumbing. But I think we can all agree that even though it was stressful, having a toilet is better than not having one. Last year, I had a major problem happen with my house, I just reminded myself I was lucky to have a house to fix.

Remember that you have the choice not to fix something that goes wrong. Choosing to fix it, means that you have decided having the responsibility for it is better than not having it at all. I would rather have pans to clean, than no dishes at all. A not so perfect job is better than having no job at all. The secret is feeling grateful, then deciding you want more and changing what you can.

Gratitude will squash any animosity that arises out of responsibility. Having responsibility is a gift. It means freedom and choices, even if things can feel out of control at the moment. Remember to feel grateful. Feel grateful that you have yourself to take care of. Someday we will all lose that right. Right now, we are alive, so we have choices, and the chance to change and that is a beautiful thing.

Recap: You have an obligation to yourself, your children and your pets. You have an obligation to make sure you have a space to call home, and what is needed to live. Your responsibilities help to make sure you fulfill your obligations. Work to pay your bills, get your children to school, and buy food to stay alive, these are responsibilities. Focus on what responsibilities can lead to your obligations and make those a priority.

"OR" and "AND"

I do have a responsibility for my children *AND* my job. But when I have to make a choice between the two and make one a priority over the other, it becomes an *"OR"* Your obligations should be the priority and win the *"OR"* everytime without guilt. These are what you obligated yourself for. Usually we can do both our responsibilities *AND* obligations. I can usually go to work, and take care of my children, but if I have to choose an *"OR"*, the obligations are priorities. And then learn to rank your priorities. In my house, my children come before my dog. I try to do *"AND"* my dog, but sometimes it is *"OR"* my dog, and I personally put my children in a higher rank on my priority list. I obligate myself to both, however all *"OR"* situations require you to make a choice for priority. Ranking our priorities is a great way to realize what we are obligated to do and how to choose our responsibilities from our priority list.

I have a responsibility to make my children dinner, because taking care of them is my obligation. I have a responsibility to make a doctor's appointment when I am sick because I am my obligation. I have a responsibility to do dishes *AND* make dinner. However, I need the dishes clean to make dinner, so this is where prioritizing comes into practice.

Now you try itemizing obligations and responsibilities and rank.

My obligations, by rank. This is what I prioritize in my life. What I will be responsible for no matter what:

My Responsibilities. This is what I choose to accomplish, but can change as life changes:

Chapter 18
Setting Boundaries and creating Limits

    Setting boundaries is one of the hardest skills we learn for life for some of us. It took me a long time to realize the importance of boundaries. This is what you are willing to tolerate as acceptable. We should all have some control of what goes on in our space. Our personal space. This is where you decide what you will allow and what you will not tolerate. If you already know what you want, and what you don't want, then decide what your boundaries are next. You almost always tolerate pet hair if you want a pet. It is hard to have the limit set on no pet hair if your animal you love is loaded with shedding hair. But I can bet most of us would not encourage our dog to poop on the floor.

Custom Shifting Cleaning and Organizing Company Presents: Home Energy

Ask Yourself:
What is my level of acceptance?

Do I have expectations in my home?

How can I change the level of acceptance to meet my desired expectations?

I have decided that in my home, I want to be treated with respect. I cannot control the outside world but I can control who is in my home. So that is my boundary. In my home, I am respected. I like boundaries better than rules. Rules seem like there is punishment if broken, or that they can be broken in the first place. Boundaries are limits that you have set. There is no smoking inside the house. That's the limit, the answer is just no. Not an "if and then", just a no.

I enforce the boundaries in my home as simple outlines. Put dirty dishes in the sink, dirty clothes in the hamper and trash in the trash can. Sounds simple to me. I don't mind if anyone wears shoes because my dog doesn't take her paws off, german shepherds get dirty, but we love her anyway. My boundaries can still be: don't leave the door open, because flies drive me nuts. I also have set the limit of what people bring into the house and leave.

Setting boundaries in your environment is easier than doing it outside our home. Starting with your space, gives you practice that you'll need for everybody and everything in life. It stems from your needs and wants. I want peace. My boundaries are no violence in my home. The more you allow what you do not want, then the less you get what makes you happy.

Practicing, learning and following through with setting boundaries can be hard at first and comes easier to some than others. I really struggled with boundaries for years, but it is more about respect. It shows the respect you have for yourself. I would not treat others with disrespect, so I should treat myself with the same guidelines in mind. The more you allow, the more you will get. I had decided when I bought my house I wanted no one to call me curse words in my space, and unfortunately, I didn't enforce it.

Eventually I asked my partner to leave because of it and now I am strict on that boundary and I live in peace at home.

Practice boundaries in your home environment because it is easier to control. You can change what you can. When you have mastered this respect for yourself, practice setting boundaries in other areas of your life. You deserve sleep, you deserve to be treated fair, and you deserve to be happy. Start treating yourself this way and set boundaries for others to treat you with the same respect. Your energy will shift when you believe you are worth it.

Decide what boundaries you could set in your home environment to make you feel how you want:

Part 2

Chapter 19
Cleaning Style

We went over how you want your space and hopefully how to get the space you want. This next section is how to keep it clean. We all need a clean space for good energy. A dirty house definitely brings our mood down, while a clean space always makes people feel happier. I understand it feels like a big task, but I have some tricks for that.

I'd like to go over an interesting thought on *how* we clean. How we are when we clean and organize can help us accomplish what we would like to in a way that works for us as individuals. This opinion I have on different cleaning styles is set to help you find your flow. Please do not label yourself or others in doing this. I have cleaned in many different personalities of homes and with homeowners. Your cleaning style might be different from your actual personality. This exercise is not to label, it is to help us find our direction.

I strongly believe there is always more than one way to do anything because everyone is different, and different approaches lead to different outcomes. Learning how we can clean and organize the way that best suits our style, is the key to turning our tasks into enjoyment.

Let's go over what I call the "Little by little,", and the "all at once approach". This is not about labeling your personality, but finding the way we accomplish our to do lists. Different ways people clean their homes. Some people work best by doing tasks "little by little", not slow in speed, but one thing at a time, usually as soon as it needs to be done. Some people work better by doing things "all at once", not faster in speed, but by jumping around with tasks. Some people can do both. Learning which method you thrive in, will ensure your best results with success.

We know there are different ways to learn in school. The visual learners learn best by watching. Cleaning is the same way, there are different ways different people thrive to clean. Just like our to-do lists. Some of us do it all at once on our day off, and some spread it over a week on our lunch breaks. Let me explain and you can decide which cleaning style you thrive in so you'll find it easier and faster and more enjoyable to clean.

I call them the "ADD" cleaning method, and the "OCD" cleaning method. There is no right way or wrong way and neither method is better. Learning the best way that suits you personally, will help you become more efficient. *The OCD style of cleaning is a little by little approach, this will be Type One. The ADD style of cleaning is explained as an all at once method, I am going to call it Type Two.*

The first step is to decide which category cleaner you are so you maximize your results. The second step is to work around your style so it's easier to clean. Remember it is not about labeling your personality, just recognizing how you like to live and clean in your home.

Type One cleaning style: Examples are the minimalist person who likes very little in their home. They are pro anti-clutter in their spaces and lives. They thrive on daily Routines. A space where everything has a "home" is ideal. The household is run more strictly with cleaning rules and they might feel very anxious in an environment that is too busy or over decorated. This cleaning type usually does tasks right away. The dishes do not tend to pile up and it is harder for them to focus if they do. They usually clean by doing one thing at a time. The whole living room top to bottom before moving onto another room. Or washing all walls in the house before moving onto floors.

Type Two cleaning style: Here are some examples of this cleaning style. This type is usually the ones who have an easy time collecting. Their space is busier and more decorated. They are laid back cleaners whose house is sometimes labeled as "lived in". Cleaning is more scattered as they are more easily distracted. Cleaning in this style is "all at once". They can pick up all the toys all over the house in every room, then get distracted by the dishes and do those. The need to fully accomplish one task before moving on to another task is not the same as the Type One cleaner. They can thrive bouncing back and forth from cleaning tasks.

Both styles are great. Doing the one that fits you, will benefit your productivity. We are all different. The Type Two style cleaner might describe the home of a Type One cleaner as "naked", "like a hotel", or even "plain". The Type One cleaner might describe the home of a Type Two cleaner as "busy", "cluttered", or "over-decorated". The type of space you want is determined by your needs and wants. A Type One cleaner might over-clean and worry too much about keeping it "perfect". A Type Two cleaner might let things go too long and lead to procrastination.

Custom Shifting Cleaning and Organizing Company Presents: Home Energy

Which Style Cleaner are you? Or perhaps a combination of both

For energy purposes, and letting go and creating the environment you thrive in, I've got some tips on how to utilize your cleaning style.

For the Type One cleaning style, learning to let go is important. It's ok to leave it undone for a minute. Try to have minimal items in your home and establish control in your environment. The Type Two cleaning style needs to focus on organization, routine, finding a place for things and decluttering.

Most people think that being a Type One cleaner can lead you to a cleaner home. Learning how to utilize my Type Two cleaning style has led me to be a super fast cleaner. I am more productive by embracing my style and working with it. I love being able to run around and clean ten things at once and multitask. My home is very busy. I love decorations. My sister does not. Her house is "simple" and has no "clutter". The point is to thrive in your environment and be happy feeling like yourself in your own space. She might clean one room at a time. I bounce around from task to task. I am more effective in using that method for my cleaning type. I am an "all at once" style cleaner. I have learned to be happy without holding onto things and I can declutter now and let go, but I like my walls to be well decorated. All I would think about with an empty wall, is filling that wall with something. That makes me a mostly Type Two cleaner, although I am both styles in a way.

So if I am the Type two cleaner, how should I clean? By not forcing myself to be the Type One cleaner. By accepting myself and embracing who I am and learning to value my differences and see them as strengths. I may be an ADD cleaner, but I am not an ADD learner. School is set up to bounce around from subject to subject. Up to six subjects a day. I do better learning just one thing at a time. So remember, just because your cleaning style might represent the "all at once", or Type Two style, do not label your personality type as ADD. I clean best by not focusing on one thing at a time. I walk by the mess on the floor and sweep it on my way to another room. I bounce around my tasks because my mind is bouncing around, and I roll with it. If I did one room at a time, it would probably slow me down.

When I clean other peoples homes, I am in routine mode. I usually do the same tasks on repeat in a routine. An auto-pilot response that breaks the mold into a more Type One habit. Anyone can develop routines. Just remember to embrace your style, accept it and thrive with it. If cleaning one thing at a time works better for you and feels more natural, do that. If you thrive on bouncing around to clean, do that. Both methods and different approaches will work toward an end result.

Just because a Type One style cleaner might appear to have a cleaner home, does mean they are happier about it than someone with a Type Two style cleaner is with clutter. They might have to stress about the mess more, and need to let go and relax. While the Type Two cleaner might have to get more routines and be more strict about the to do list. It's about accepting yourself and deciding what you want out of your environment and how to attain that, not labeling yourself as "not good enough".

We are all different and can be whoever we want to be in our own environment. Change what you can and what you want to change. But recognize who you are and work around your strengths. The most important choice to remember is to give yourself credit for what you accomplish.

Little by little: Type One
Do I have to finish a task before moving onto the next?

Do surfaces with "things" make me anxious?

Do I tend to have less stuff?

Would you prefer simpler or controlled walls?

All at Once Cleaner: Type Two
Do I move onto other tasks before finishing?

Am I easily distracted in my home?

Is my home "busy?"

Do I have a lot of decorations in my home or like to collect?

There is no right way to clean. Type One tends to do things as they need to be done, dishes after dinner. So the Type Two cleaning style needs to focus more on routine and setting a time built in to do these tasks. I now clean my fridge and cat box every Tuesday because the trash comes wednesday. I am mostly a Type Two cleaner, so setting a time aside makes it part of my routine.

Tips for Type One cleaner:
Set routines for tasks like laundry
Try cleaning one room at a time
Cut down on distractions and clean with the TV off
Keep it simple: Do sheets one day, walls next
Utilize closets for storage
Do it when you think it

Tips for Type Two cleaner:
Keep baskets to hold odds and ends and put away when it is full
Clean in layers
Play music, and ebook or talk on the phone while cleaning
Embrace the ability to multitask
Allow yourself to move around and cross off as you go
Keep closets and hiding places for stuff at a minimum

No matter what style cleaner you are, remember that your way can work and does not have to be the same as someone else's. It is your home and as long as you are committed to change and celebrating yourself without comparing yourself to others, you will achieve your goals. Eventually I got better at doing my tasks "right now" which is the method that has worked best for me.

Chapter 20
Keeping it all clean

I had to add this section because I'm a professional. I have seen lots of homes and they are all different. Different homes for different people. I'm going to give you some great pointers so you can clean your house the way you like it. I talked about clutter and how it affects your space. Seeing the surfaces of counters and shelves, floors and tables make every space look instantly better. The number one tip I can give is clean counters and clean floors. If the only task I ever did was vacuum, the space would look ten times better. If floors and counters are clean your house will look better.

Vacuuming can be so much work so hire out if you have to. But do not skip floors. Typically as a cleaner, I do bathrooms and floors. When you are in your space, this makes the most difference. We are usually on the floor walking and we always use the bathroom. So we'll start with those first. If you are going to vacuum all the floors, you have to be able to find the floors first. That is why cleaning the floors is the most important.

I love a good vacuum with a hose to get under and around. But everyone has a different skill level so know your limits. For some surfaces a swiffer works great. To save money you can just use shop towels and you can wash the towels after. This trick works for high shower walls and house walls and ceilings as well depending on the surface. I also like to use the swiffer to clean under beds and furniture too if the vacuum hose does not reach.

The trick is to wipe your upper surfaces onto the floor before you clean the floor. It is the easiest approach. Top to bottom. No point in washing countertops then taking cobwebs down from the ceiling onto the clean countertops. Dusting walls and ceilings does not have to be done often in most homes. It does however, make the whole house look cleaner when done. But we're here to start small first. Do those dishes in a routine. Write on your schedule a time to vacuum. If you physically cannot do the labor of most of the chores, remind yourself that it is ok to hire out.

Keep in mind the effort and labor that goes into cleaning and maintaining a household. It keeps people in business to hire out. House cleaners work hard and deserve respect. They are definitely earning their money. Even if you price out a housecleaner and think it is too expensive, put it on your priority list to afford and then figure a way out to afford it. Maybe you never watch your cable or could save money on your gas by rideshare. Maybe you could trade services with someone.

If you can physically clean your home to your liking then it is a great workout and the exercise is good for your body. Either way feel accomplished that you are getting it done. And please respect the energy it takes to clean by others and appreciate and respect their service to you. It is hard work and those of us that work for ourselves do not earn sick time off either. But the service is worth the price if you need help, so respect and appreciate and receive the assistance.

The best advice I can give is cleaning top to bottom. Wipe all surfaces this way so you don't have to repeat the process. Make the bed before the floors. Spray the whole toilet and wipe from lid to seat to base. Top to bottom. Don't vacuum until the top surfaces are all wiped. *Saving time means saving energy and that leaves more time for more energy.* Some of your chores get added to the routine list. I went over that in time management. Some accomplishments are done a few times a week, or every other week or even once a month. I do not often wash my curtains. That isn't even on my schedule until around christmas.

    I love the idea of making the bed as soon as you wake up. If this is possible to make a habit out of making your bed then that is great. You will feel better because it is done. A bed that is made makes the whole room feel better and ready. It might be easy for those of us that are so busy to just keep cleaning wipes in the bathroom and just wipe the toilet every few days. Some people clean as we go, some clean all at once. That comes to your cleaning style. Cleaning the whole house at once takes a lot more energy at once.

    When I clean other's homes I clean the house top to bottom all at once. It takes hours sometimes of non stop movement. This works in my customers homes, but in my own home it is harder for me to focus on just cleaning straight through. In my case, the routine of a little by little approach works better for my schedule sometimes, but I have gotten better at both styles. I take down the cob webs when I see them. But it does not make sense to do this after you have already cleaned the floors.

    Some surfaces we forget about. Our lights and ceiling fans can hold a lot of dust. Those can be done as needed and don't need a routine. Your fridge will make you so happy if you clean it. The best way to make your house look better is floors, usable surfaces, and what we see the most. If your bathroom is dirty every time you use it, it will drain your energy. I also went over excuses or reasons.

I will be the first to tell you that when I wrote this book I realized I didn't think I had the time or energy to keep my house clean. So I made a choice to start my journey towards a new job. I was too physically burned out cleaning all day in other people's homes to clean my own. I also did not make enough money to hire my own housekeeper. So I made the choice to get a new job because the energy was draining me so much worrying about my to-do list that I was procrastinating. So I understand the struggle and it is not easy to make changes sometimes. But the right changes will make you feel better and improve your positive energy in your home, environment, lifestyle and change your mood and how you feel about your life. So it is worth it to change what you can.

Start by telling yourself you will clean the floors only. Then know you should wipe the surfaces first. You should also pick up anything on the floor first. When the floors are clean you will feel better about your space and your accomplishments. Keep in mind there is no shame for hiring out. I have a lawn guy because my push mower gives me carpal tunnel. The company is worth it to me. I hired a mechanic because I do not have the tools or knowledge to fix my car. I still consider that I have accomplished getting my car fixed. There is zero shame in hiring someone to do bathrooms and floors in your home. Just remember they are worth the money you are paying.

I mop floors "on my way out", meaning I do not walk over the floor until it is dry. Always mop with the direction of the wood and keep your mop moving left to right or vice versa, not all over in a circle. I use a junk credit card for scraping off services with excess filth. They make razor blades for glass windows and stovetops. Once in a while, don't forget the light switches or door handles.

If you plan on cleaning your own home on an every week or day basis, I have some tips. Make cleaning fun and rewarding. Do it when you can look forward to it. Play your favorite music and dance while you work, or listen to an ebook on your headphones. Make it less of a chore and more of an accomplishment. Please make sure to remind yourself of your success and achievement because the work is a choice not a curse.

Remember to take something out in trade if you bring something in so that things in your home do not pile up. After you work hard to get your home the way you'd like, you do not want to start over and have to declutter again. Try as best as you can to get onto a routine that is accomplishable. Some days our priorities change and that's ok, just try to stick to a schedule that you can hold yourself to.

Also, remember the importance of communication. Communication is important for every aspect in life. The most important person you need to communicate with is yourself. Ignoring what you are trying to tell yourself is like your child telling you they are sick and ignoring them. It is not fair or respectful so make sure you are communicating with yourself. If you are thinking you should do something, do it. Listen to yourself the way you would your children. You deserve that respect, so trust your intuition.

Chapter 21
Tricks of the Trade

Not everyone can be a speed cleaner, and that is totally understandable. We can, however, all be successful. I have learned some secrets running a cleaning business I would love to share now with no competition.

Bathroom: Just wipe down the sink and counter after you use the bathroom, then it will always be clean. Always mop the bathroom last unless you use a separate towel or mop. It is a huge pet peeve of mine working in a restaurant to see the mop being used in the bathroom then dragged over the rest of the floor space. If you think about it, it is pretty gross. "Push" the toilet water down with the brush before you clean it. You can force the water below the usual toilet water line to clean the ring around it. Clean toilets before the sinks. Top to bottom.

Wash what is dry, and dry what is wet: Good rule to follow. Dry the surfaces that are always wet, such as the sinks, and tubs. Wet the areas like the outside of the toilet and floors, windows and counters. Of course if you have time or energy, then drying the surface after would be ideal. But the best way to keep your tub clean is to keep it dry sometimes. It is the constant wet surface that will make it harder to clean in the future. Try not to use too strong a chemical as a habit in your tub. If you have to rinse what you are using to make it safe, try using something different instead. No one wants to bathe in Ajax. It is not good for your skin. Would you want to use the same wet towel for a week? No, it would smell. Standing water gets gross too, just like the washing machine will get an odor if not left open once in a while.

General clean: Seriously vacuum everything. If all you did was vacuum, you could clean everything. Consider your vacuum like your favorite tool for success. You can use the hose to vacuum all your surfaces in your house pretty much. Vacuum the furniture, the baseboards, the bottom of the toilet, the heat vents, the lamp shades, window sills. Vacuum everything you can, suck up the cobwebs. There is no chemical in the vacuum, it just sucks up. It can be your magic wand if you use it correctly, and it definitely is a workout. If you have a shop vac, you can even get the hair out of your tub before you clean it. The broom is great for taking down hard to reach cobwebs, but the vacuum is the tool that does it all. You can even vacuum your mattress with a hose. If you can vacuum your whole house, then all you have to do is wipe some surfaces off and Voila!

Delegate a laundry time in your home. Most of us have clothes to wash, fortunately. Everyone in the house should have their own hamper and if possible, wash the load that is in the hamper and then you know whose clothes they are. Get a system. Wash your clothes on sunday for example, kids on a tuesday, or whatever works, but get a system because laundry is huge and can be overwhelming.

Throw the junk papers away at the post office before you even leave. If you have a mailbox, sort them immediately. The bills that come in, write on the calendar a few days before they are due, and attach the bill close by for reference. Keep your papers in your "office" space. Everyone should have a to-do thinking space, even if it is super small. The need for us all to own computers gets bigger by the day.

Keep shoes in a shoe cabinet, or shelve or closet. They do look like clutter and they are usually full of dirt. Also, use an area rug to trap dirt coming into the house so you can shake it off outside.

Cover or hide surfaces you can't change and that bring bad vibes. Put a cover over the stained couch for example. I am not a fan of hiding things, but the point is to change what you *can*. If you really cannot change the hole in your floor, right now, there is duct tape and an area rug for a reason.

Also, try not to use furniture that is way too big for your current space. No point in a huge couch in a studio apartment when you might be able to use a daybed instead that serves functions.

Recycle, Reuse and Repurpose every chance you get. Use the kitchen table for art, use the old carpet under the mulch outside. Rearrange the house and use the toy shelf for a tv stand, be creative and use what you have if it works. If you have moved something three times and it still does not have a home in your space, pass it along. No need to store items you won't use. Mason jars are a beautiful way to store so many items like brushes, art supplies, food and toiletries. You can wash them when they get dirty, but they do look great when used as storage.

Organizing and keeping your items can be so fun when using what you already have if you can.

Use separate hooks for bath towels, backpacks and jackets and use labels if possible. None of these items belong on the floor and I always tell my kids that only our feet belong on the floor. I repeat those boundaries often. Keep kitchen counters clear. I know they can be a caught-all, but even a basket by the door can work for lost items. Just make sure to empty the basket when it is full. Our whole kitchen looks clean with clear counters. And most fruit is better in the fridge anyway because we all dislike fruit flies.

Add things to your virtual cart when shopping online, and hit the save for later, this eliminates impulse buys and allows you to save what you wanted, but give you time to consider if you really want to bring it into your home, also you will notice most items do not expire, so there is no rush.

And go ahead and spit your mouthwash in the toilet. It does kill germs right?

Chapter 22
Cutting Corners

It is definitely true that we all fall short on time or energy sometimes, or motivation and still have a to-do list. Cutting corners doesn't always mean skipping what you need to do, but it might relieve some of the pressure. I am a natural multi-tasker but I am still working on routines. Remember we can't make time, but we can save time.

Some Tips for Speed:

*Delegate some takes out if you can, ask for help or hire

*Have pizza for dinner, it is okay to skip making dinner sometimes and go with takeout

*Use paper plates. If your dishes take forever, use those paper plates sometimes to save energy

*Use automatic food and water dishes for the pets, you might only have to fill once a week instead of everyday

*Set out clothes outfits for the week on Sundays or your day off

*Make lunch for tomorrow the night before if possible and refrigerate

*Do online banking, waiting at the bank can take forever, try using the app or ATM if possible, banks are always busy friday afternoon

*Order Walmart groceries and household items to be delivered at your door if possible, it saves me worlds of frustration personally

*Use the crock pot for dinner, they also make crock pot bags to make clean up a breeze

*In a pinch you can use Ziploc bags for leftovers

*Braid your hair before bed, it saves you time in the am

*Fill the gas tank to the top, why stop more than you have to, and pay at the pump if possible

*Set up automatic bill pay, just make sure to write on your calendar the date bills are removed so you can make sure the money is in your account

*Make your dinner schedules so they can blend with other days or prep ingredients at once, like cooking two pounds of burger at once for spaghetti one night and tacos the next.

*Send emails while you are waiting in line or in the waiting room

*Make your own ice and bring your own water bottle

*Make appointments long before you need to, that way you'll have the flexibility to change it if you have to. Don't wait to schedule your checkups, dentist or car appointments. These places are scheduled out for a long time.

*Go to quick oil change places. I've had good luck with them and I clean the interior of my car while I wait

*Do that five minute shower, you can get clean in five minutes if you wanted to

*Clean your house and skip the gym, cleaning is such a workout

*Throw on that hat, hats are cute no matter what hair you have or don't have

*Use blankets or covers for furniture, you can just wash them, but it saves the furniture

*Get a white board or chalkboard for your house. Write down the to-do list, shopping list or reminders in a place you'll see it.

*Set reminders on your phone a few days before someone's birthday or event so you are prepared

*Push all the dirt towards the floor before you vacuum

*Put a small trash container or bag in the car

*Multi-task your errands. Like drop the dog off for a bath and go make that trip to the store

*Order half of your presents for others online, but buy good deals if you see in person

*Use an old fashioned calendar, never hurts to have one on the wall

*You don't have to wash your hair everyday unless it gets really greasy

*Send virtual invites for parties, take a picture of it and text

*Label your seasonal decorations on their tote

*Bring that magic eraser in the shower with you and never "clean" the shower separately again, just wipe down when you see it in the shower

*Turn off social media at least once a week or skip it on your phone

*Let the kids play video games or watch TV sometimes if you have chores to do. Kids Youtube is not the best, but it is a tool we can use if we have to

*Run your errands during the least busy time of day, never between 4-6 when most work gets out

*Place small trash cans in multiple rooms and hampers in every bedroom and change once a week in routine

*Keep an extra outfit in your car for everyone in case you have somewhere unexpected to go

*Always keep a prepaid Visa for at least fifty dollars in your wallet for emergencies

*Start Christmas shopping in October, holidays should not be a stressful time, and you'll beat the shipping rush and crowds

*Travel when most people are not going. Pull the kids out of school if it's worth it

*Set the clock in your car and home ten minutes fast and train yourself to go by that time, you'll be earlier and feel less stress

*It is okay to buy in bulk the items you use a lot of. Trash bags etc, just make sure you have the room to store them. It is easier to budget if you only buy trash bags once a year.

*Always stash a few gallons of water in case the power goes out, (if you have space in the garage) it'll save you running around in a hurry

*Have baby wipes just in case in your car and house. There is hundreds of uses for these, taking off makeup, washing your hands, cleaning, dusting etc

*Proportion meat and freeze it, label it with a to-use-by date with a sharpie on the bag

*Use mason jars for fruit to keep in the fridge. Those grapes are ready to eat if you prepare them

*Put your toppings on the frozen pizza arranged to cut before you bake so it's easy to divide

*Put your dirty dishes in the dishwasher as soon as they get used and label them with a magnet "dirty", if you are lucky enough to have a dishwasher, or wash immediately by hand.

*Put your requests for vacations and day offs at work as far in advance as possible in writing. This will save you the stress later

*Always keep a medicine kit with first aid and tylenol and covid tests if you need them. You never know when you will need childrens meds, and sometimes the supply is actually limited, and who really wants to make an official store trip if they are sick?

*Store away a cell charger, maybe batteries and a lighter, and a pen just in case, you'll save energy later without worrying.

*Keep a notepad and pen on your night stand and write down what you are thinking before bed and cannot sleep.

* Keep a paper copy of your call contacts in an address book, it's just handy if you lose your phone

*Go ahead and write down your passwords on paper stored in your house. Is someone really going to break into your home to steal those? No, they can do that digitally if they want.

*Keep a list of the companies you pay bills to and the date they are due and the phone number to call them. Someone else might need this information one day. This includes a list of all your credit cards and the contact number on the back. If you ever lose your wallet, this will save you so much time.

*Write emergency numbers on your fridge. It's hard to think so fast under pressure.

*I have used Affirm for years to finance my kids christmas presents, I pay off every year and start again. Not having to budget everything in my schedule reduces my stress

*Always keep your resource list handy. Make a list of plumbers, carpenters, neighbors, vets etc.

*Pay attention to local drop off and transfer station days or donation days. Once a month, take a pile down you have "traded".

*Use baskets for "clutter" and empty it when it is full. Most of it you'll realize you do not need

*Splurge on a few extra cell chargers and keep them in your busy parts of your home. Bedroom, living room and kitchen.

*Use an old fashioned calendar. It;s the only way to visually see quick what our responsibilities look like.

*Communicate with yourself about decisions so the regret of not doing it, will not take up extra space in your mind

*Pre-pay for heat if possible. Winter is expensive and stressful enough

*Set alarms for "bedtime". We set them for the morning routine

*Do what you think you should do

*Put your car keys in the same spot. I bring them up when I am sleeping and have a hook when I am home awake.

*Set your morning alarm ten minutes early

*Check the weather. I subscribe to the weather channel app on my phone. We can't control the weather and it does affect our lives

*Load virtual coupons to your phone and use your phone number at checkout, because why not

*Set out your clothes for the next day the night before

*Write your weekly to-do lists on your fridge and calendar

*Menu plan before you write a shopping list, you might not need now what you are out of

*Do your tasks before they are due because something always comes up

*Set yearly schedules on monthly habits, such as: October: Christmas shop, july: prepay fuel. Etc...

*Don't buy a years clothes at once, buy a few and replace throughout the year

*Budget what you need for yourself monthly, like one month hair done, next month ebook, etc

*Make time for friends. Even a phone call a week changes our mental state.

*Make sure you leave time for yourself, even if you have skipped a "chore". It is priceless use of time

*Trust your judgment the first time and listen to your intuition.

Being prepared for some events will eliminate time and stress from your life, just as long as you're not always worried about it. Some things weigh us down if we keep, but some give us peace of mind. Every home should have a first aid kit and a storm emergency kit.

Chapter 23
Products

I have some advice on what products you should spend your hard earned money on and which you should avoid. Do whatever you like in your home, this is just my advice coming from a professional cleaner.

I think I have tried every product or close to for cleaning. I am not promoting any one product, however using products professionally is different from home use. I spent a year coughing like crazy because I was spraying products in my eyes and nose all day. So I have a good idea of what works the best for me now. This is my opinion and not advice for you. I do speak from experience though running a cleaning business.

Bleach: honestly one of my least favorite chemicals to use. It burns your eyes and your lungs when you use it. You shouldn't need anything this strong routinely in your house. You are not cleaning a hospital with other people's blood. Please don't use such strong chemicals that you fry your brain cells. Just because it "smells clean" does not mean it is healthier for your body. Straight Bleach to me is not an everyday go to and should be used in moderation. I do however love the Clorox brand of cleaning wipes, the Scentiva Coconut and Waterlily. I can't help it, they are brilliant. But a stronger spray is fine to keep in the cabinet in case someone gets the stomach bug for some reason.

Windex and vinegar: Use windex when you feel you have to. I am not a fan of spraying too much windex because it does breath into my airways. Seriously, just use some vinegar and water mixed together. One of my older clients swears by using newspapers instead of paper towels. Also, a handy trick with vinegar is scent removal. I used it all over the house when my dog got sprayed by a skunk.

Peroxide: Really good for toilets. It is not as toxic if you have a dog who drinks from the toilet (luckily I don't, but no judgment) and you can pour on the toilet brush instead of spray.

Murphy oil and spray: I love the spray. It is multi-use and great with wood. It claims it is almost all natural and smells great. I spray on a cleaning cloth and not on the surface and I have never had a problem with damaging surfaces. I use the oil in my mop bucket to clean other people's floors. It smells great and does not make me cough.

Dawn: I think this is the best dish soap to wash with. When I mop my own floor, I actually use dawn dish soap and I boil my water before I pour in the mop bucket. I add a few drops of dawn to the hot mop water. Sure boiling water is slightly dangerous, but if your floor can tolerate super hot water then it is less scrubbing. They use dawn on birds so I consider it safe. I wash my makeup off with dawn so I stick to that label for life. Try adding a drop of essential oil to your mop water such as peppermint.

Magic erasers: So much debate on this one. I do use them because they work. It is elbow grease as my Gram used to call it or it is less scrubbing. It's your house, your decision. It is your space and environment. Personally I use them for walls, tubs, sinks, doors and even sneakers. They call them magic for a reason. While I try to make a positive impact on the earth, this book is about cleaning and not saving the environment as a whole. Agree or disagree, but they work.

Simple Green: Ok, I have been using this for years. I love that you can mix it to concentration according to your needs. The smell is nice and subtle and I have used it on so many surfaces with a positive experience. I have even used it on glass windows and mirrors. I clean my toilets with simple green spray and my shower. I am definitely not getting paid to promote the product so I am just recommending from my personal experience. I add a drop of essential oil to my simple green and use it on most all surfaces. I have even removed carpet stains with this stuff.

I talked about the *swiffer.* There are a bunch of brands out there. Just look for one that has the ability to tuck in the towel. Then you can save money by using cleaning wipes or microfiber cloths instead of having to purchase over and over the floor wipes they sell. Sorry to the companies for saying that, but they are expensive. Two of those clorox wipes I talked about earlier, the scented ones, work like a floor wipe if you're not too frustrated in it splitting halfway through. Otherwise you can use a cloth and wet or spray it for the hard to reach places.

What if you have no spray? Well go ahead and squirt some of your hand sanitizer on the toilet and wipe off and watch it shine. If it sanitizes your hands, it should work on the surface of the sink too.

O- Cedar: This mop all the way. Spin it drier and go. When you're done, take it off and wash it. From my years of working in the restaurant business I have nightmares about the wet mop smell, so I can't smell that smell personally. Makes sense to me to clean with a clean mop, so I stick with this mop head. You can even use a clean dry mop head to dust hard to reach places like under beds or crown molding or ceiling trim.

Oils: If you have your surfaces clean then oil can help them shine. White mineral oil really does work for stainless steel. A good stainless steel product has white mineral oil. A good wood oil has some sort of oil such as orange oil which is a favorite of mine. A stone cleaner has some oil in it. Oil shines surfaces up, and the same is true for your hair or face. I use Weiman products for the stone spray and stainless steel. I can't help it, they smell great.

Bar keepers friend: Not sure why but this stuff works. It does wonders on my old sink to remove rust stains and now comes in a spray that I have definitely used to remove hard water stains from the inside of toilets. Handy to have on hand. Just like any product, read the label and use according to directions.

Baking soda: I am sure there are a million uses for this. I refresh my cat litter boxes and sprinkle on the rug before I vacuum. Not a bad idea to leave pretty vases of this stuff around in the bathroom for scent removal. I have used it with vinegar to unclog my drain before although so many reports say it might be bad for your drain. I am not an expert plumber, but I have used straight baking soda to wash clothes in my washer. I have also brushed my teeth with it so I consider it safe. I know you can clean your tub with it because bath bombs already contain it anyway without a disclaimer.

Vacuum: I have gone through dozens of vacuums in my years of professional cleaning. I have never found one brand I love for every surface. I like vacuums with hoses because they get corners and under surfaces. I only use Hepa filters to protect my lungs. I also try to never buy the vacuums with the California Prop Warning. There are plenty of brands out there without that disclaimer.. I have not seen any difference in my house cleaning abilities by using a fifty dollar vacuum or a five hundred dollar vacuum. Marketing has so much to do with it.

There are a bunch of good stick vacuums for those who like light cleaning and these work fine unless you have a ton of dog hair like I do. You shouldn't need a beater bar unless you have wall to wall carpet, but keep in mind what a workout it is to pull a heavy powerful suction vacuum. Personally I like shop vacs because you can go over most wet areas and use it to unclog your drain. To get the best out of your favorite tool, get a lighter vacuum with a hose that is easy to use and make the cord longer with an extension cord if you want. Make sure it has a filter and clean it so you don't make your dust airborne. If anyone makes the world's best vacuum, send me an email, I'll try it.

Chapter 24
Problem Areas

Mold: I want to start with my least favorite which is mold. Mold is so nasty for your health. It is bad for your lungs and your brain and never creates a positive environment to live in. Unfortunately it is natural and occurs without us inviting that in. Go ahead and use those strong smelling chemicals designed to "kill" it, just wear a mask and gloves and air the place out. Keep in mind though that mold will return until the problem is fixed. Mold likes moisture. So even if the mold is gone, it can return. The problem stems from a bigger issue. I can't give you advice on removal but I can advise you to remove it. Mold can affect you in such negative ways if not taken care of.

Grout lines: If I had a dollar for every time I tried to explain to someone that grout is not waterproof. You can bleach grout, but it will never stay forever. It is porous unlike most tiles used to tile. Consider eventually regrouting. It is a pain to grout, my least favorite part of tiling, but eventually it fixes the problem longer. You can use a grout pen to fill in the grout on the lines. Do what makes you feel better on this one. Excessive scrubbing removes grout and without grout in between the tiles, it can create mold on the wall or surface behind the tiles. Some stains cannot be removed with cleaning products from porous surfaces and have to be removed or covered up. Think painting a wooden table. You would have to sand the table or cover it with a tablecloth, most grout is the same way.

Pests: I am talking about ants, mice, bugs etc. They do not make good energy in your home if they are unwelcome guests. I try to go as natural as I can on this one. There is no way to sugar coat though that mice dropping are extremely unhealthy and should not be around where we eat and sleep. So many solutions claim to remove them and if there is a big problem please call a professional. They do this for a living and they are experts in their field. Sometimes hiring an expert is just the best choice. Make sure when cleaning up mice droppings you use gloves and a mask. I go with the solution of having cats. Cats work for me but they don't work for everyone. Then you have to make sure to clean up after your cats too because cat urine is so unhealthy to breathe in as well.

I believe in peppermint oil as a deterrent for pests. I love the way it smells and pests generally do not like the way it smells. I have also heard cinnamon works for ants. Neem oil for outside I have used as well. They say pick up all food sources too but honestly I have seen the cleanest houses struggle with ants or mice. These pests are small and find a way in and can bring in their own food. So I think I want my space to be inviting for me and my friends and family but not all become a roach motel for pests. The point is don't live with it. Hire a professional if necessary or reach out for help. Your space should be free of the stress of the dangers that these pests bring with it. Good energy comes from a healthy living environment. Healthy physically and emotionally and mentally.

Stains: Typically if we cannot get the stains out of objects, it is a reminder of why it was stained. Focus on that memory for one minute. If we can remember and let go of anything, we do not need to to hold on to it. We do not need to keep that stain. Even if you do not realize it, you think about it every time you see it. The same goes for anything broken. You do not need to keep broken items to remember why it broke. The point is to learn your lesson and move on. If you are keeping broken or soiled or ripped items, you just need to learn the lesson, love it and let go. It really does drain your energy to save. That is my advice. The rug the dog peed on over and over, let it go.

My friend Linda, is a master fixer, I think she could fix anything. If this is you, that is great. Some people love to fix things, for others we just store this in the "to fix" portion of our space and do not get to it. For years, I had saved clothes I planned on sewing to fix. If you know you do not have the time to commit to that energy, let it go. It is not a priority for me anymore.

My sister always reminds me that the definition of insanity is doing the same thing over and over and expecting a different result. Everytime we hold on to broken items we are secretly telling ourselves that we don't deserve new things. The only thing we should be attempting to fix everyday is ourselves. We can let go of material things. It is the memory that matters. If it isn't fixed, and the stain cannot be fixed, replace it and let it go. Create new memories in peace and joy. Would we save a broken balloon because it used to have air?

Smell: This is huge. Nothing like walking into a house and smelling an unpleasant smell. This could make all the difference in the way you feel and think. Scent has the power to make us think differently. I believe in this so much that I started my new business around this belief.

What are your favorite smells?

It would help to really think honestly about this and make a list. Most smells are attached to memories or feelings. The feelings in that memory. I personally like the smell of fresh baked apple pie. It reminds me of when I was a child and we all got together for the holidays and shared hugs and happiness. It is a good memory and thus a good feeling. So my brian in turn associates this as a good smell.

No one feels better when they smell trash or cat urine. I love the smell of flowers because it reminds me of the open fields I grew up in. They were so safe and peaceful. Not many people would buy a puke scented shampoo, so this makes sense. The smell of popcorn reminds me of my mother. Still to this day she loves popcorn.

Please make a list of scents that you love and the feelings they bring to you. If you have a memory attached to this scent, great, but you don't need one. Just a feeling of peace or joy or calm or clean work too. Most people associate orange and lemon with a clean house for some reason. Of course my house can't always smell like apple pie, or I might eat too much sugar. But I love the smell of fresh brewed coffee because I love coffee. The point is we all love the smell of something. Some smells bring negative feelings without us even thinking about it. No one wants to walk into a home and smell gas or smoke. Those smells promote fear and anxiety and therefore not a peaceful environment. I hide our cat litter box in a cat box piece of furniture making it functional and less smelly.

Custom Shifting Cleaning and Organizing Company Presents: Home Energy

Our home's smell should welcome us and invite us and make us feel happy. What are some scents that you love and bring positivity to the way we feel and think.

Favorite scents: *Feeling I feel:*

Chapter 25
Our senses

It is hard sometimes to smell our own house. I often smell other people's homes and don't realize my own. Is it a wet dog, dust, a library smell, or the dirty sink smell? The strong smell of tide? Which I personally don't like at all. It's a smell I don't prefer because I want my clothes to be just clean and not smell like laundry soap, mainly because I like to smell like my own perfume instead.

Either way it is easier to list what we want our smell to be first. I want my house to smell peaceful and restored. Energetic yet peaceful and full of joy and promise. Change comes from making a decision to want more, setting boundaries to accept no less and the action to make it happen.

Please make a list of the words you decided your house should feel. And I'll walk you through how to get that smell. Peace in your space does not just come from sight, it comes from scent and feel too. Get those cozy soft blankets and throw pillows. Feel the space, see the space as peace and breathe in the peace. I make my own line of room sprays and house and car scents for this reason. I went into business doing this because I truly believe in the power of scent. Please feel grateful to be you if you can smell, it is definitely a gift and should be exercised. More people can smell than can see without assistance. It is an overlooked power we have to change the way we feel. Some days I want to feel empowered. Some days I want to feel refreshed. But I always want to feel peace. I have personally decided that in my own journey because peace and safety are important to me.

So peace is on my list. Maybe a house that smells fresh is yours, maybe high energy or focus or calmness. Everyone is different. Remind yourself that your space does not have to smell like bleach to be clean. It can smell like jasmine and be clean too.

I love fresh flowers, flowers are so visual and such a bonus if they smell good too. I have a rose in a vase in the bathroom. Buy yourself a single flower you are not allergic to and try it. I love admiring the rose's beauty everytime I go to the bathroom. I usually only stop running when I am in the bathroom and that gives me a chance to see and appreciate the amazement of the flower. Carnations are my favorite flower and like daisies, will change color when you add food coloring to its water. It is definitely acceptable that I added a drop of rose scent to my flower vase. Honestly a bathroom is the perfect place for flowers. Having three kids made me realize how often I visit the bathroom and it is the most popular place for guests to look around as well. Also try oil diffusers.

In our home we love soft objects. My kids love soft blankets and warm floors because they run barefoot. Our dog loves fuzzy surfaces so I have area rugs. Area rugs are my personal favorite because they can change the feel of a room in seconds. Do not overlook the power of the sense of touch when making your home *you*. I like the idea of leather couches but I am not a fan of how it feels, so my couches are covered with soft covers that I can wash.

Recently, we had to quickly leave our home to visit a sick friend out of state. I was rushing around nervous trying to leave. Somehow I knocked over a bottle of essential oil I had on my mantle. When we returned later in the week I was shocked by how great the house smelled. I feel peace walking in; being invited by the smell of exotic flowers changed my mood and lifted my energy.

Sound is another sensory issue addressing some spaces. Some homes are on busy streets with busy neighbors and we cannot change the outside world. Brainstorming ways to fix the space so it suits your comfort is a great way to start. Thick curtains or a water fountain feature, or even a box fan or tranquil music. There are ways to avoid the distractions of unwanted noise. Even a noisy fridge can be distracting at times. Try to pay attention to your sound as well. I love music, so playing music in my home makes me feel positive, and free.

We went over the emotions of the home you want, now try these senses by brainstorming your favorites:

Sound I want in my home:

Smell I want in my home:

Sights I want in my home:

Touches I want in my home:

Chapter 26
Essential Oils

Essential oils are so powerful for us mentally and spiritually they can change the way we feel. The power of scent is that important. Let's go over a few associations so you can better choose a scent for space if you need to be refreshed.

Popular Space smells:	The Why:
Orange, lemon, citrus	We think clean and fresh
Lavender	Calming and reduces anxiety
Peppermint, Eucalyptus	Relieve congestion and help us breathe
Vanilla	Comforting, inviting
Floral scents	Happiness, relaxation
Cinnamon	Creative, focus

We use these scents sometimes without thinking. Our cleaners have an orange scent and we put lemons in our sinks. People use Vicks for colds and have flowers for joy. I bet a lot of people have bought those cinnamon brooms they sell around the holidays. It becomes an association with what we smell and what we think of when we smell it.

I do love the smell of holiday candles burning as I love candles to begin with. There is a feeling you get when you walk into a house with a candle burning a warm yummy scent and it fills the room. Also, the flame is visually calming. Candles are a great way to enhance the energy in your space. I did however leave most of the popular candle scents off the list because I really don't need to be reminded of food in my house while I am in it. I personally prefer to cook the food instead. But the apple, pumpkin and blueberry scents are amazing.

I personally want my house to invoke good memories and feelings without the association of convincing me to eat more. I have a sweet tooth so although I love apple pie scent, I do not burn that candle in my home. I guess I would rather cook the pie sometime. My personal choice is floral and peppermint for its benefits to my body and home. But everyone is different so do you in your space.

I believe strongly in candles to enhance space. Fire when used correctly is part of the natural elements and does invoke peace to watch the little flame. Candles have been used since the beginning of time for sight and warmth and now we use them for scent. Every home should have at least one candle, even if you don't light it. They come in handy if you need them. Candles are associated with celebrations. This is why we light a candle on a birthday cake and make a wish. Our brains associate candles as a happy thought, and the scent that comes from that can make us happy too. Our space should be a positive place to release our energy and to be ourselves and encourage who we are to burn bright like the light we are.

If burning candles is not an option for you in your space for some reason, there are many options for scent release now. I love the burners and oil diffusers. I got a beautiful one from my sister for Christmas that lights up and changes colors and I add some water and oil to it to enhance my calm. I use my organic and safe room spray to give each room the vibe I want. I have the calming for my bedroom and the citrus and cinnamon for my kitchen. I use the floral in my bathroom, and peppermint is always somewhere in the house. You can place a few drops of peppermint around the baseboards hidden on cotton balls to reduce pests. Mine are usually behind the couch. I just swear it works, but again I have cats.

Spraying some room spray works great. I have the best luck spraying on something. I've sprayed my curtains, and my rugs. Do not use aerosol please. The typical bathroom spray you buy at the supermarket is artificial with chemicals and not good for your body. Anything aerosol is bad for your lungs, and what we breathe should be as fresh as possible. I do have a line of room sprays that I can't live without for my car. I love keeping a bottle of my spray in my car. Remember that candles are a great addition to a home. If you can not burn the candle, leave the lid off.

Without a doubt I truly believe in the power of burning sage. It really does help clear out negative vibes and increase positive energy. All spaces probably need a good sage burning once in a while and I definitely notice a shift after I burn sage. I use white sage but I like sage in general and I always keep some handy in my house. If you have not tried sage, please do. If you feel like you need a fresh start, sage is the way to go.

It also helps to set an intention when you burn the candle. Say and think "peace" and light that candle. Whatever you believe you need, set your intention and believe in it. I swear by the power of intuition and holding space in our body's for our mind's desire.

Chapter 27
The Elements

The importance of including the elements in your home is so immense that I could write a book on just this subject. I'm going to touch on the why and keep it simple. Since humans existed, we have depended on the elements and the way they coexist with us is crucial to our survival. Placing as much variation in your home creates a natural peace in your space.

Earth: The power of plants. Plants are so important for any space. There are hundreds of house plants with each having a different cause and effect. I love Rubber plants because they help remove impurities from the air. Spider plants are a popular choice. The visual effect of plants is unlimited. Just please make sure to research if the plant you choose is safe for your pet and your allergies if you have them. They are living and create life and most of the time require little assistance to survive. Even if you grow some herbs in your window, it creates meaning and responsibility and purpose. Incorporating Earth into our environment brings peace and connection.

Fire: I just went over why I think every house should have a candle. This is a simple way of introducing a positive element into your home and when used safely can reduce stress and promote relaxation. Fire kept humans alive for centuries and is a part of all of us naturally and spiritually. People still gather around a fire for celebrations and warmth.

Water: No one can survive without water, water is just that important. Not everyone can have a fish tank like I do, and we do love our fish tank in our home. Luckily there are so many water features that allow for the movement of water in our homes. Everyday I feel grateful for the water and love the sound it brings to my space. Even a small water feature works in your home.

Metal: Definitely one of my personal favorite decorating tools. I love metal. I have metal candle holders on the wall to hold my curtains back and a metal coffee table. It does not have to be a big piece but I bet we all have some metal already in our homes. Our bed frame or silverware perhaps. I bet if you look around your space you'll see some metal already, maybe your cabinet pulls or door handle. Metal is so much better than plastic. Plastic really is toxic.

Wood: Wood keeps us alive in so many ways. Our house is made from wood, the trees are wood. Wood is nature, strength and endurance. It can keep us warm and protect us and it is renewed by the earth. Wood is nature's gift and should be kept, accepted and appreciated.

Air: Air is also what we need to survive. We can only go minutes without air before we leave this earth. So the air in your space should be clean, safe and comfortable. I love air purifiers, I have used them in my home since I moved in. My house is super old and drafty and I love the clean air that comes from air purifiers. Clean air is better for our body and makes for good energy in our home. Some devices also make a "white noise" sound that I personally love. But clean air should be the top priority in your home because we breathe there, and breath is life.

Custom Shifting Cleaning and Organizing Company Presents: Home Energy

Incorporating the Elements into our space, brings balance and good home energy.

Chapter 28
Feng shui

I do believe as a designer in Feng Shui, and because I could write an entire book on interior design itself, I will try to just lay out some basics. Someone will always roll their eyes at Feng Shui, but it creates an energy and movement and flow to your space so it is important. I know not everyone can move windows and doors to make their space more "energy efficient", but even small decorating changes can shift the energy in our space.

If you have a compass, use it for this exercise.

That water element I talked about earlier is best placed in your home in the north to create abundance and good fortune.

The Metal element should try and face West in your home.

The wood Element should be used on the East side of your home.

The fire element in your home should be South side facing. This all helps to create balance in your home. There are so many compasses you can find that have multiple decoration directions, so I kept it easy.

This should be easy to achieve if you get creative. A painting or sculpture works just fine as an element. I just try to avoid excess plastic, I believe that plastic can be mimicked as estrogen and no one needs added hormones. Colors can also be used to represent the elements if you prefer colors instead. Be creative and enhance your personality with design placement.

Air exchange is like energy movement and should be allowed to flow through your space uninterrupted. The windows and doors of a home are where energy flows in and out of. The hallways are better left open as are the entryways of doors as much as possible to allow for movement of energy.

I am a firm believer in placing a mirror in every room, although the advice is not to place a mirror on a wall that faces a window. Think energy bouncing off and leaving. Mirrors are great in a home and can create more light and distance when placed correctly. They are also said to ward off evil spirits and who wouldn't want that?

The earth element I used to reference is plants and if possible, please use houseplants. I think they add life to homes and purpose and rebirth. They help to clean the air and bring positive vibes into a home. Read about your plant, and put them in your home wherever they will flourish. The more the better. I miss having a house full of plants, but my cats keep eating them. Even the bathroom looks nice with a cactus, if you can pull off those touches with your space.

Chapter 29
Lighting

Lighting is another subject I could write chapters on. Honestly it does deserve its very own little section at least. Nothing changes the feel of a room as much as light does. It is something we can control most of the time and has a direction shift on our mood and the energy in our space. I prefer brighter lights that dim. Play around with direct and indirect lights to suit your comfort.

I have heard some people say that overhead lights give them a headache, I have never had a problem with this though. I love fairy lights as I call them, the lights on a string that can be turned on when the main light is off. I love the look of these around the top of the room near the ceiling. This creates a different atmosphere for relaxing later in the day when the main lights are too bright. Remember that Halogen bulbs are a bright light and Incandescent bulbs are warmer. I do like brighter lights in my bathroom to put my makeup on, and I prefer softer lights in the living room for relaxing.

Lighting can create such a mood in your space. At night, my kids like to use the star lights on the ceiling for relaxation and comfort. A good idea as well is motion sensored night lights because the overhead light might be too bright in the middle of the night. So many light fixtures to choose from, so many styles from industrial to modern to recessed. If you can't change out your fixture, adding an option for a floor light is a great choice. Play with the placement so the shadows do not interfere with your activities.

Think about what is important to you in your home and add the necessary light to transform your space. Do you need a writing nook light? I am a huge fan of salt stone lights because of their beauty and function. Of course natural light is always the best choice, so having curtains you can close and open is a great idea for any space when privacy is desired. But in general, darker rooms set the mood for winding down and make you sleepy, so not a great choice for productive spaces.

If we are lucky enough to be able to see, then we should enjoy the energy that light gives us. Light is literally energy, making it so important to our home's vibe. Loving the candle you lit and enjoying the flame is a great way to enjoy energy at its finest. Especially in the winter when it is more dark and cold, light helps to boost a mood.

Chapter 30
Colors

I am sure everyone has a favorite color or color pallet that they are drawn to. Everyone might have a different version of what neutral means. For some, it is white, off white, tan or gray. Mine is gray, I do love that color. Colors can bring mood in a space and affect the energy. Have you ever been in a bright orange room? I bet that would be distracting and busy and too much for most. The color would be hard to not notice or feel something while you were in it.

I learned in a great college class at Goddard College about color theory. It is amazing how the surroundings of a color can change the way that color looks. Have you ever picked out a color swab and noticed the paint on your wall did not come out how you thought? Maybe that green color now looks mustard yellow. The colors reflect off different surroundings and other colors and light to bring out undertones of their relative shades.

A color with a mood not in line with your needs, might have a negative affect on your home's energy. Peeling cracked paint or no paint at all might be dragging you down without knowing it. Try and change what you can to uplift your mood. I try using contrasting colors in my decor, such as gray and yellow and blue. Some people stick to all the same shade of gray or brown. It is wise to choose a color to add some energy to your space to fit your desires.

Blue creates the mood of joy and calm
Yellow creates excitement and energizes
Red is known to show power and hunger for life
Gray is balanced and neutral
Brown is earthy and stable
White is a blank slate and more open to change, looks "clean"
Green creates the mood of relaxation
Black color is bold and strong

The colors you use to enhance your space depend on the mood you are going for. I am a blue person and always have pops of blue because it reminds me of a beautiful sky. If you cannot paint your walls, throw pillow, rugs and blankets are a great way to accent any space.

Wallpaper has made a comeback and there are so many versions out now and can be used to divide spaces and create the illusion of a separate space. Think back to your list you made in the beginning of the course on what you wanted out of your space. Could a rug be used to divide the space, or color on an accent wall? It is your space and should reflect you.

Remember the importance of the use of color in your space. Changing what you can means you can change the color scheme and enhance your space to fit your personality. Be aware of the mood you are trying to set and what you are trying to gain from your new space.

Changing any color in your space, will change the energy or mood of that space.

Chapter 31
Motivation

I have told my clients not to be alarmed when we start to deep clean and change the space if more problem spots seem to be noticed out of nowhere. After washing the floors, you might notice that the cabinets are dirty. This is actually progress and should not be discouraging. If this happens, it is because you are losing your "slight blind" for your space and that is **Change**. Once you start cleaning and changing things around your house, you might notice more that needs to be done and hopefully you are motivated to keep going.

Hopefully you'll have some ah-huh moments where you notice what has gone unkept or un-noticed. Owning a cleaning business made me realize how much I directly impacted the moods of my clients. When your home is clean, you do feel better, it is that simple.

Practice these skills in your home, your happy place:
Realizing what you want in your home

How you want your home to feel

What the energy in your home feels like

How you want to be treated in your space

What are your favorite hobbies

The colors and scents that make you feel happy

Your relationship with time

The boundaries you are willing to set in your home

Your personal ability to let go of what does not belong

Setting your routines for accomplishing you tasks

Feeling grateful for your responsibilities

Accepting yourself and celebrating it

Deserving respect for yourself

Loving the space you are in

Now I please ask you to practice these skills in your home, your own personal space, then take these skills to other areas of your life. Learn to embrace what you have practiced in your career, your relationship with others and your relationship with yourself.

Allow your change to be your motivation. Dance in your home if that is what you enjoy, always look back to the words you used to describe your dream home and keep that handy to remind yourself of your goals.

One day I was cleaning my fridge and took out a shelf to make more space for bigger items like milk and juice. The change was amazing and everytime I opened my fridge, I was happy and calm. Change can be that powerful.

What if you went through this whole course and changed what you could and you still think you can't make your space to fit what you want? It happens. Sometimes we just realize who we are and what we want and what we have is not what we want. That is perfectly fine, now you can have the goal of getting what it is you do want. Eventually I want a mountain view because it was my favorite part of my childhood and makes me happy. And I made a goal to someday get that mountain view. I am grateful for my home now and I have done my best to be happy and appreciate my space. My house serves me for my values, and my style and my likes and wants, but someday I am getting that mountain view because I know now I deserve it. And you can do the same. You can get what you want if you make it a priority and believe you deserve it.

I want to help you realize that if you were like me, constantly trying to change your environment over and over, and it was never good enough, that is because you lack the change elsewhere in your life. I can promise that your environment is the easiest thing you change, but it is only the stepping stone. It is important after trying to change your space to realize where else in your life you might feel out of control and where else you could change. Practice with your home, but keep your skills to set a value and feed the energy you create to re-establish boundaries and control in the rest of your life. Please learn to change what you can when you need change, and keep in mind, your environment might not be the only place you are craving change. Believe in yourself, respect yourself and be the change you need. For you *are* different.

If I can do it, so can you.

Chapter 32
Be Yourself

Remember that little quiz on Cleaning Styles where you were assessing your cleaning style. You might have the same decorating style as cleaning style. They could be opposite, but perhaps it gave some idea of the style you like to keep in your home. Recognize your decorating style and celebrate your space with your personality in mind.

If you like a simple house, with empty walls, please keep a simple house. The point is to make your house your space. If you're like me, and like a very decorated house, then by all means decorate it. Please do not do what you think will be appealing to others in your home. This is your house you are planning, and changing for the better for you.

Setting boundaries means you don't need to take it personally if someone tells you that you have too many plants. Please do you and your style. Whatever was on that list for your needs and wants in the beginning of the course should be what you set your goals around. Your hobbies and your interests and your personality. Being yourself and expressing yourself and accepting who you are will always bring positivity and good energy into your space. There is freedom with self expression and the joy that comes from not hiding and being true to yourself is worth all the effort that energy it takes you to accomplish.

Your house can be your happy place, your space to grow and thrive with acceptance and respect. I believe in you and you should believe in yourself. I am proud of you for taking the steps to change what you can and control what you can. Your energy will shift if you believe you deserve to be happy and accepted and free from judgment in your space. Setting boundaries and following through with your goals will get you to the end result you strive for.

Change starts with realizing that you want to change, then making a decision to make that happen. The action is fueled by the drive in the belief that you can control what you can. You can control your energy in your space. You do have freedom to choose and decide your personal environment. Being grateful for the choice means being grateful for the responsibility and the ability to take that action. I am so honored to have encouraged you to celebrate and respect yourself. You deserve it.

Congratulations on your path and good luck on the journey. A new adventure is always a choice away, a change away from the shift. Love yourself and the space you are in for everyone is different and you are the only you. CustomShifting@outlook.com

Chapter 33
Resources and Research

Deciding what you want is the hard part, getting it should be achievable. Do not be afraid to reach out for help now if you need it. Here is some tips to brainstorm:

*Check with your local newspaper or advertising website for listings on local cleaners. Licensed and insured businesses might seem safer, but use your judgment.

*Compile a list of free donation places around your area, mine are Restore, Salvation army. Our local transfer station also takes metal for free so get creative.

*Research a list of where you can sell your items. I have a Facebook marketplace that I post my kids' clothes on, but there are also websites that are local to each area as well for listing unwanted items.

*When in doubt, a "Free" Sign by the road might work to get something gone.

*Reach out to your community action or state agency on assistance for resources. Every state has multiple organizations that assist with information. So much can be learned simply by asking.

*Usually every town has a bulk trash pickup or drop off once or twice a year. Call the town managers in your town to find out.

*Ed2Go and IAP career college have so many interesting classes to take to broaden your horizons and hobbies if you unsure of your current career

*Reach out to your doctor for advice if you feel like you are lacking mental or physical capabilities to achieve your desired happiness.

*States have an information hotline with resources to call with questions, ask and you might receive

*So many colleges, training programs and vocational centers have volunteers who are learning a trade and might be able to help. When I was in Cosmetology school, we offered services at a huge discount and dental schools typically do too.

*Ask a school for resources. They might know students who need passive income, or community service hours or even a family who might be looking for something you are donating. Some schools keep extra jackets for children who lose or forget theirs.

*Check homeless shelters to see if they are in need of any household items you might have. Even rehab or people leaving corrections might need some free household items that you now can donate and not throw away.

*Reach out to your friends for advice. The right friend will point you in the right direction

*Check your local library or church and keep track of local events and fundraisers that you might be able to donate your unwanted household items to

*Go to an "open house" for a house on the market, notice what you like about the space and how it feels and looks just to get ideas

*Research your hobbies for classes offered in your areas. You might even meet people with similar interests

*Check electronic stores to see if you can donate old electronics, or if they might have information on where to go for that

*See if you can trade resources with someone. Maybe you are a childcare provider and they mow lawns and perhaps you could trade services.

*Check out workshops and community events that are going on for ideas and inspiration

*Visit showrooms and furniture stores for inspiration. They often have whole rooms set up as stages for design.

*Ask questions!

*Coming Soon: Our new line of homemade products DaretoThere perfumes, sprays and candles for personal energy adjusting to help you continue on your journey.

Thank you so much for reading. I am truly honored to inspire you,

Love and respect always,
Christyna